Talking Love

Proven Strategies for Better Communication in Relationships

MICK BELL

The presentation of the information is without contract or any type of guarantee assurance. The trademarks that are used are without any consent, and the publication of the trademark is without permission or backing by the trademark owner. All trademarks and brands within this book are for clarifying purposes only and are the owned by the owners themselves, not affiliated with this document.

Table of Contents

Chapter 1

Introduction

The Importance of Communication in Relationships

Effective communication is the cornerstone of any healthy relationship. It serves as the bridge that connects individuals, allowing them to share their thoughts, feelings, and needs. Without clear and open communication, misunderstandings can arise, leading to conflict and resentment. This chapter delves into the importance of communication in relationships, exploring how it helps build trust, resolve conflicts, and foster a deeper connection between partners.

Trust is the foundation of any strong relationship, and communication plays a critical role in establishing and maintaining it. When partners communicate openly and honestly, they demonstrate a willingness to be vulnerable and share their true selves. This openness fosters a sense of security and reliability, as each person knows they can count on the other to be truthful and forthcoming. Trust is not built overnight; it is cultivated through consistent and meaningful interactions. By regularly expressing their thoughts and feelings, partners can build a solid foundation of trust that can withstand the challenges that inevitably arise in any relationship.

Conflict is a natural part of any relationship, but how it is managed can make all the difference. Effective communication is essential for resolving disputes in a constructive manner. When partners engage in open dialogue, they can better understand each other's perspectives and work together to find a solution. This requires active listening, where one partner fully concentrates on what the other is saying without interrupting or formulating a response in their mind. Active listening shows respect and validates the other person's feelings, which can defuse tension and pave the way for a resolution.

Moreover, clear communication helps prevent misunderstandings that can lead to conflict. Misinterpretations often occur when individuals assume they know what their partner is thinking or feeling without actually asking. By explicitly expressing their thoughts and emotions, partners can avoid these pitfalls and ensure that they are on the same page. This transparency reduces the likelihood of miscommunication and helps maintain harmony in the relationship.

In addition to resolving conflicts, communication is vital for fostering a deeper emotional connection between partners. Sharing personal experiences, hopes, and dreams allows individuals to bond on a more profound level. This emotional intimacy is crucial for a fulfilling relationship, as it creates a sense of closeness and mutual understanding. Regularly discussing both the mundane and significant aspects of life helps partners stay connected and engaged with each other's worlds.

Nonverbal communication also plays a crucial role in relationships. Body language, facial expressions, and tone of voice can convey a wealth of information beyond words. Being attuned to these nonverbal cues can enhance understanding and empathy between partners. For instance, a warm smile or a gentle touch can communicate love and support, while crossed arms or a furrowed brow might indicate discomfort or frustration. By paying attention to these signals, partners can respond more appropriately to each other's needs and emotions.

Effective communication also involves being aware of and managing one's own emotions. Emotional intelligence, or the ability to recognize and regulate one's emotions, is key to healthy interactions. When individuals are in tune with their feelings, they can communicate more effectively and avoid reacting impulsively in heated moments. This self-awareness allows for more thoughtful and measured responses, which can prevent conflicts from escalating and promote a more harmonious relationship.

Another important aspect of communication in relationships is expressing appreciation and gratitude. Acknowledging and valuing each other's contributions can strengthen the bond between partners. Simple acts of expressing thanks or recognizing efforts can go a long way in making each person feel appreciated and valued. This positive reinforcement encourages more of the same behavior, creating a cycle of mutual respect and kindness.

Communication is not just about addressing problems or sharing deep emotions; it also includes the everyday interactions that make up the fabric of a relationship. Small talk, playful banter, and shared laughter all contribute to a sense of companionship and joy. These light-hearted exchanges are just as important as serious conversations, as they build a sense of camaraderie and shared enjoyment.

It is also important to recognize that communication styles can vary significantly between individuals. Cultural background, personality, and past experiences can all influence how a person communicates. Understanding and respecting these differences is crucial for effective communication. Partners should strive to be adaptable and open-minded, finding a communication style that works for both parties. This may involve compromising and finding a balance between different preferences and habits.

In some cases, communication in relationships may be hindered by external factors such as stress, fatigue, or external pressures. It is important to recognize these influences and address them accordingly. Creating a supportive environment where open communication is encouraged can help mitigate these challenges. This might involve setting aside dedicated time for meaningful conversations, reducing distractions, and prioritizing the relationship amidst busy schedules.

Technology has also changed the landscape of communication in relationships. While it offers new ways to stay connected, such as through text messages, social media, and video calls, it also presents challenges. Misunderstandings can arise from the lack of nonverbal cues in digital communication, and the constant presence of technology can sometimes detract from face-to-face interactions. It is important for partners to find a balance, using technology to enhance their communication while also making time for in-person conversations.

Ultimately, the importance of communication in relationships cannot be overstated. It is the lifeline that keeps partners connected, allowing them to navigate the complexities of life together. By prioritizing open, honest, and respectful communication, individuals can build stronger, more fulfilling relationships. It requires effort and commitment, but the rewards of a deep and trusting connection are well worth it. Communication is not a one-time task but an ongoing process that evolves with the relationship. By continuously working on their communication skills, partners can ensure that their relationship remains strong, resilient, and enriched with mutual understanding and love. Beyond the foundational aspects, communication in relationships also involves addressing specific needs and preferences. Each person in a relationship has unique desires and expectations, and expressing these clearly can prevent feelings of neglect or dissatisfaction. Whether it's about personal space, emotional support, or shared responsibilities, openly discussing these aspects can help partners meet each other's needs more effectively.

How to Use This Book

Navigating the landscape of personal development and growth often requires a roadmap, a guide that can illuminate the path ahead. This book is designed to be your companion on this journey, providing insights, tools, and actionable steps to help you achieve your goals. Understanding how to use this book effectively will maximize its impact on your life. Here's how you can make the most out of each chapter and transform the knowledge within these pages into tangible results.

Begin by recognizing that this book is structured to build progressively. Each chapter is crafted to address specific aspects of personal and professional development, leading you from foundational concepts to more complex strategies. To fully benefit from this approach, it is advisable to read the book sequentially. While you might be tempted to jump to sections that immediately catch your eye, starting from the beginning and moving through each chapter in order will ensure a comprehensive understanding of the material.

As you read, take an active approach to your learning. Passive reading can lead to information slipping through the cracks, but engaging with the content actively will help you retain and apply what you learn. One effective method is to keep a journal or notebook dedicated to your journey through this book. Jot down key points, personal reflections, and how you plan to implement the strategies discussed. This practice not only reinforces your learning but also serves as a valuable resource you can revisit.

Each chapter includes practical exercises and prompts designed to help you apply the concepts to your own life. Don't skip these exercises. They are integral to the learning process, turning abstract ideas into concrete actions. For instance, if a chapter focuses on goal setting, take the time to outline your goals, create actionable steps, and set deadlines. These exercises are not mere add-ons but essential components that bridge the gap between theory and practice.

Reflection is another crucial aspect of using this book effectively. At the end of each chapter, pause to reflect on what you have learned. Consider how the information relates to your personal experiences and current challenges. Ask yourself questions like, "How can I apply this concept to improve my daily routine?" or "What changes do I need to make to align with these principles?" By engaging in this reflective practice, you deepen your understanding and make the content more relevant to your life.

Additionally, this book emphasizes the importance of consistency and persistence. Personal development is not about quick fixes but about gradual, sustained effort. As you work through the chapters, commit to implementing the strategies consistently. It may be helpful to set aside regular time each week to review what you've learned and assess your progress. This consistent effort will yield cumulative benefits, leading to significant improvements over time.

Another way to enhance your experience with this book is to connect with others who are on a similar journey. Whether it's through discussion groups, online forums, or study partners, sharing your insights and challenges with others can provide support and additional perspectives. Explaining concepts to someone else is also a powerful way to solidify your understanding. Consider forming a small study group where members can discuss each chapter, share their reflections, and hold each other accountable for completing exercises and implementing strategies.

Remember that setbacks and challenges are part of the process. As you apply the principles from this book, you may encounter obstacles or moments of doubt. It's important to view these not as failures but as opportunities for growth. Each challenge you face is a chance to test your resilience, adapt your strategies, and learn more about yourself. Keep a positive mindset and remind yourself that growth often comes from overcoming difficulties.

Incorporating feedback is another vital element of your journey. As you implement the strategies from this book, seek feedback from trusted friends, mentors, or colleagues. They can provide valuable insights into your progress and offer suggestions for improvement. Be open to constructive criticism and use it as a tool for further development. Remember, the goal is continuous improvement, and feedback is an essential part of that process.

To further enhance your learning, consider supplementing the material in this book with additional resources. Books, articles, podcasts, and seminars on related topics can provide deeper insights and broaden your understanding. This supplementary material can also offer different perspectives and techniques that complement the strategies discussed in this book. Create a personal development plan that includes a variety of resources and experiences to enrich your journey.

It's also beneficial to set specific goals for what you want to achieve by using this book. These goals can be related to various aspects of your life, such as improving your communication skills, enhancing your productivity, or fostering better relationships. Clearly defined goals will give you a sense of direction and purpose as you work through the chapters. Regularly review and adjust these goals based on your progress and evolving aspirations.

Lastly, celebrate your achievements, no matter how small they may seem. Personal development is a journey, and acknowledging your progress along the way is important. Each step forward, each new skill acquired, and each challenge overcome is a testament to your growth and commitment. Celebrating these milestones will boost your motivation and reinforce the positive changes you are making.

In conclusion, using this book effectively involves a combination of sequential reading, active engagement, practical application, reflection, consistency, collaboration, resilience, feedback, supplementary learning, goal setting, and celebration of progress. By embracing these principles, you can transform the knowledge within these pages into meaningful action and lasting personal growth. This book is a tool designed to empower you, and your active participation is key to unlocking its full potential. As you continue your journey with this book, remember that personal development is deeply personal. What works for one person may not work for another, and it's important to tailor the strategies to fit your unique context and needs. Flexibility and adaptability are key. If you find that a particular approach or exercise isn't resonating with you, don't be afraid to modify it. The goal is to find what best supports your growth and aligns with your values.

Setting Relationship Goals

Setting relationship goals is a powerful tool for fostering healthier, more fulfilling connections with others. Just as personal or professional goals provide direction and motivation, relationship goals can help you and your partner grow together, address challenges, and build a stronger bond. Whether you're in a romantic partnership, nurturing friendships, or improving family dynamics, setting clear, actionable goals can transform your relationships.

The first step in setting relationship goals is to reflect on what you want to achieve. Consider the current state of your relationships and identify areas where you see room for improvement. This might include communication, trust, intimacy, or shared activities. Reflect on past experiences and what you've learned about your needs and your partner's needs. Understanding these aspects will help you set goals that are meaningful and relevant.

Once you've identified areas for improvement, it's important to have an open and honest conversation with your partner. Share your reflections and listen to their thoughts and feelings. This dialogue should be a two-way street, fostering a sense of collaboration and mutual respect. Effective communication is the foundation of setting and achieving relationship goals. It's essential to approach this conversation with empathy and a genuine desire to understand your partner's perspective.

Specificity is key when setting relationship goals. Vague goals like "improve communication" can be difficult to measure and achieve. Instead, aim for specific, actionable objectives such as "schedule a weekly check-in to discuss feelings and concerns" or "dedicate 30 minutes each evening to unplug and connect." These clear, concrete goals provide a roadmap for action and make it easier to track progress.

Another crucial aspect of setting relationship goals is ensuring they are realistic and achievable. Ambitious goals can be motivating, but they should also be attainable given your current circumstances. For example, if you both have demanding jobs, setting a goal to spend every evening together might be unrealistic. Instead, you could aim for quality time on weekends or during specific evenings when you're both free. Setting achievable goals helps maintain momentum and prevents frustration.

Flexibility is also important. Relationships are dynamic, and circumstances can change. Be prepared to revisit and adjust your goals as needed. Regularly check in with each other to discuss progress and any new challenges that may have arisen. This ongoing dialogue allows you to stay aligned and make necessary adjustments to your goals, ensuring they remain relevant and attainable.

In addition to setting goals for improvement, it's beneficial to set goals that celebrate and reinforce the positive aspects of your relationship. Acknowledge what's working well and find ways to build on those strengths. For instance, if you both enjoy a particular hobby, set a goal to do it more often together. If you have a tradition that brings you closer, make it a point to maintain and cherish it. Celebrating these positive aspects strengthens your bond and adds joy to your relationship.

One effective strategy for achieving relationship goals is to break them down into smaller, manageable steps. Large goals can feel overwhelming, but smaller steps make the process more manageable and provide a sense of accomplishment along the way. For example, if your goal is to improve communication, start with small changes like actively listening during conversations or setting aside time each day to talk without distractions. These incremental steps build a solid foundation for achieving larger goals.

Accountability is another important factor. Just as with personal goals, having someone to hold you accountable can significantly increase your chances of success. In relationships, this means both partners need to take responsibility for their roles in achieving the goals. Regularly discuss progress and gently remind each other of your commitments. This mutual accountability fosters a sense of partnership and shared purpose.

While setting and working towards relationship goals, it's important to remain patient and compassionate. Change takes time, and setbacks are a natural part of the process. Approach challenges with a problem-solving mindset rather than blame or frustration. Celebrate small victories and remind yourselves of the progress you've made. Patience and compassion help maintain a positive atmosphere and keep you motivated.

In some cases, you may find it helpful to seek external support. Couples therapy or counseling can provide valuable guidance and tools for setting and achieving relationship goals. A trained professional can offer an objective perspective and help you navigate challenges that may feel insurmountable on your own. Therapy can also provide a safe space to explore deeper issues and develop healthier patterns of interaction.

Building and maintaining healthy relationships requires ongoing effort and commitment. It's not a one-time task but a continuous journey of growth and adaptation. By regularly setting and revisiting your relationship goals, you create a framework for ongoing improvement and connection. Remember that the ultimate aim is to enhance your relationship and bring you closer together, not to achieve perfection.

Incorporating shared activities and experiences into your relationship goals can also strengthen your bond. Plan activities that you both enjoy and that allow you to connect on a deeper level. This could be anything from traveling together, taking up a new hobby, or volunteering for a cause you both care about. Shared experiences create lasting memories and reinforce your connection.

Finally, it's important to balance relationship goals with individual goals. Healthy relationships thrive when both partners also pursue their personal growth and interests. Encourage each other to set and achieve individual goals, and celebrate those successes together. Supporting each other's personal growth enhances your relationship and adds to the richness of your shared life.

In conclusion, setting relationship goals is a powerful way to foster growth, connection, and fulfillment in your relationships. By reflecting on your needs, communicating openly, setting specific and realistic goals, and maintaining flexibility, you create a strong foundation for ongoing improvement. Celebrate your strengths, break down goals into manageable steps, hold each other accountable, and seek external support if needed. Approach the journey with patience, compassion, and a sense of partnership, and your relationships will flourish. Remember, the process of setting and achieving relationship goals should be a source of joy and connection rather than stress or pressure. It's important to approach these goals with a positive mindset and a shared commitment to enhancing your relationship. Celebrate your successes together, no matter how small they may seem, and take time to enjoy the journey.

Chapter 2

Understanding Communication

The Basics of Communication

Understanding the basics of communication is crucial for fostering healthy and meaningful relationships, whether in personal or professional contexts. Effective communication involves more than just exchanging information; it's about understanding the emotions and intentions behind the words. It requires active listening, empathy, and the ability to express oneself clearly and respectfully.

One of the fundamental aspects of communication is active listening. Active listening goes beyond simply hearing the words being spoken; it involves genuinely paying attention to the speaker, understanding their message, and responding thoughtfully. This means putting away distractions, maintaining eye contact, and showing that you are engaged through nodding or verbal affirmations. An effective listener also reflects on what has been said, asking clarifying questions if needed, and summarizing the speaker's points to ensure mutual understanding.

Empathy is another cornerstone of effective communication. Empathy allows you to connect with others on an emotional level, which is essential for building trust and understanding. When communicating, try to see things from the other person's perspective and acknowledge their feelings.

Phrases like "I understand how you feel" or "That sounds really challenging" can validate the other person's experience and demonstrate that you care about their emotions and point of view.

Clear and concise expression is equally important. It's essential to articulate your thoughts and feelings in a straightforward manner, avoiding vague or ambiguous language. Being direct yet respectful helps prevent misunderstandings and ensures that your message is received as intended. For instance, instead of saying, "I'm upset with how things are going," you might say, "I felt hurt when you didn't include me in your plans." This specific feedback helps the other person understand the exact issue and work towards a resolution.

Non-verbal communication also plays a significant role in how messages are received. Body language, facial expressions, gestures, and tone of voice can all convey powerful messages, sometimes even more so than words. Being aware of your non-verbal cues and interpreting others' can enhance your communication skills significantly. For example, crossed arms might indicate defensiveness, while an open posture can suggest receptiveness and openness to dialogue.

Another important aspect is the ability to manage and resolve conflicts constructively. Disagreements are a natural part of any relationship, but how you handle them can make a significant difference. Effective communication involves addressing conflicts calmly and respectfully, focusing on the issue at hand rather than personal attacks. Use "I" statements to express your feelings without blaming the other person, such as "I feel ignored when you don't listen to my opinions," rather than "You never listen to me."

Timing also matters in communication. Choosing the right moment to have important conversations can affect the outcome significantly. Avoid discussing sensitive topics when either party is tired, stressed, or distracted. Instead, find a time when both of you can be fully present and focused on the conversation. This consideration can lead to more productive and positive interactions.

In addition to these skills, cultural awareness is becoming increasingly important in our globalized world. Different cultures have varying communication styles, and being aware of these differences can improve your interactions with people from diverse backgrounds. For instance, while some cultures value direct and explicit communication, others might rely more on context and non-verbal cues. Understanding and respecting these differences can prevent misunderstandings and foster more effective communication.

Feedback is another critical component of good communication. Providing and receiving feedback constructively helps improve interactions and relationships. When giving feedback, be specific, focus on behaviors rather than personal traits, and offer suggestions for improvement. Similarly, when receiving feedback, listen without becoming defensive, and view it as an opportunity for growth. Phrases like "Thank you for your feedback, I'll consider your suggestions" demonstrate openness and willingness to improve.

Emotional intelligence (EQ) is also integral to effective communication. High EQ involves being aware of your own emotions, managing them effectively, and recognizing and influencing the emotions of others. People with high emotional intelligence can navigate social complexities with ease, leading to better communication and stronger relationships. Practices such as mindfulness and self-reflection can enhance your emotional intelligence, making you a more effective communicator.

Assertiveness is another valuable communication skill. Being assertive means expressing your thoughts, feelings, and needs directly and honestly while respecting others. It's a balance between passivity and aggression. Assertive communication helps you stand up for yourself without alienating others, fostering respect and understanding. For example, instead of passively agreeing to something you don't want or aggressively rejecting it, you could say, "I appreciate the offer, but I'm not able to take on this project right now."

Storytelling is a powerful tool in communication. Sharing personal anecdotes or relevant stories can make your message more relatable and memorable. Stories can illustrate points, evoke emotions, and foster a deeper connection with your audience. When using storytelling, ensure that your stories are relevant and concise, and that they support the main message you're trying to convey.

In professional settings, communication skills are crucial for collaboration and productivity. Clear and effective communication can prevent misunderstandings, streamline processes, and enhance teamwork. Regular check-ins, clear instructions, and open channels for feedback are essential for maintaining effective communication in the workplace. Additionally, being able to communicate your ideas persuasively and confidently can advance your career and help you achieve your professional goals.

Effective communication also involves knowing when to communicate. Sometimes, the best approach is to listen and observe rather than speak. Being attuned to the situation and the needs of the moment can help you decide when it's appropriate to contribute and when it's better to hold back. This discernment can prevent unnecessary conflicts and enhance the quality of your interactions.

In summary, mastering the basics of communication involves active listening, empathy, clear expression, non-verbal awareness, conflict resolution, timing, cultural sensitivity, constructive feedback, emotional intelligence, assertiveness, storytelling, and situational awareness. By developing and honing these skills, you can improve your interactions, build stronger relationships, and navigate social and professional settings more effectively. Communication is an ongoing process of learning and adaptation, and with practice and dedication, you can become a more effective and impactful communicator. In addition to these foundational skills, it's important to recognize the role of technology in modern communication. With the rise of digital communication platforms, such as email, social media, and instant messaging, understanding how to communicate effectively in these mediums is essential. Digital communication often lacks the non-verbal cues present in face-to-face interactions, making it easier for messages to be misinterpreted. Therefore, clarity and precision are even more crucial when communicating online. Use clear and concise language, and consider the tone of your messages. Emojis and punctuation can help convey tone, but they should be used appropriately and sparingly to avoid misunderstandings.

Verbal vs. Non-Verbal Communication

In any interaction, communication can be broken down into two fundamental types: verbal and non-verbal. Both play crucial roles in conveying messages, emotions, and intentions, yet they operate in distinct ways. Understanding the interplay between these two forms of communication is essential for anyone looking to improve their interpersonal skills.

Verbal communication involves the use of words to share information. This can occur in various forms such as face-to-face conversations, phone calls, written correspondence, or even virtual meetings. The primary advantage of verbal communication is its ability to convey complex ideas and detailed information precisely. For instance, during a business meeting, discussing project details verbally allows for immediate clarification and feedback, which can be vital for ensuring everyone is on the same page.

However, verbal communication is not solely about the words spoken. The choice of words, tone of voice, and pace of speech all contribute to how the message is received. A simple phrase like "I'm fine" can have different meanings depending on whether it's said with a cheerful tone or a somber one. Thus, mastering verbal communication requires not just a good vocabulary but also the ability to modulate tone and pace to suit the context.

Non-verbal communication, on the other hand, involves the transmission of messages without the use of words. This includes body language, facial expressions, gestures, posture, eye contact, and even the physical distance between communicators. Non-verbal cues often convey emotions and attitudes more powerfully than words can. For example, a person might say they are confident, but if they are slouching and avoiding eye contact, their body language tells a different story.

One of the most powerful aspects of non-verbal communication is its ability to convey feelings and emotions. A smile, a nod, a furrowed brow—these can all communicate a wealth of information about a person's emotional state without a single word being spoken. Non-verbal cues often operate subconsciously, both in expression and interpretation. This means that people can pick up on these cues without actively thinking about them, which can make non-verbal communication a more honest form of expression.

The interplay between verbal and non-verbal communication is where the true complexity lies. Often, non-verbal cues can complement, enhance, or contradict verbal messages. For instance, during a heartfelt apology, maintaining eye contact and a sincere tone can enhance the credibility of the words spoken. Conversely, if someone says they are happy for you but rolls their eyes, the non-verbal cue contradicts the verbal message, leading to confusion or mistrust.

To become an effective communicator, it's important to align verbal and non-verbal messages. Consistency between what is said and how it is said increases the likelihood of the message being received as intended. This alignment builds trust and reinforces the communicator's credibility. For example, if you are giving a presentation and you say you are excited about a new project, your enthusiasm should also be evident in your gestures, facial expressions, and tone of voice.

Active listening is a skill that integrates both verbal and non-verbal communication. It involves fully concentrating on what is being said rather than passively hearing the message. Active listening includes responding with appropriate verbal feedback, such as paraphrasing or asking questions, and non-verbal feedback, such as nodding, maintaining eye contact, and leaning slightly forward to show engagement. This combination of verbal and non-verbal cues demonstrates to the speaker that you are fully engaged and value what they are saying.

Cultural differences can significantly affect both verbal and non-verbal communication. Different cultures have varying norms and practices regarding how messages are conveyed and interpreted. For instance, in some cultures, direct eye contact is a sign of confidence and respect, while in others it can be perceived as rude or confrontational. Similarly, the use of space and touch can vary widely.

Understanding these cultural nuances is crucial for effective communication in multicultural settings. It requires not only awareness but also adaptability to modify one's communication style to respect and align with the cultural context.

In professional environments, mastering both verbal and non-verbal communication is essential for leadership, teamwork, and conflict resolution. Leaders who can effectively use both forms of communication are better equipped to inspire and motivate their teams. They can articulate visions clearly and back them up with confident body language and expressions that convey enthusiasm and commitment. In teamwork, clear and consistent communication fosters collaboration and trust among team members. When conflicts arise, the ability to communicate both verbally and non-verbally in a calm and constructive manner can facilitate resolution and maintain relationships.

Non-verbal communication can also be leveraged in negotiations and persuasive contexts. Subtle cues like mirroring the body language of the person you are negotiating with can create a sense of rapport and trust. Maintaining an open posture and using hand gestures to emphasize key points can make your arguments more compelling. Being aware of the other party's non-verbal signals can provide insights into their thoughts and feelings, allowing you to adjust your approach dynamically.

In personal relationships, non-verbal communication often plays a more significant role than verbal communication. Intimate partners rely heavily on non-verbal cues to express affection, empathy, and support. A comforting touch, a warm embrace, or a shared smile can convey deep emotional connections that words alone might struggle to express. Being attuned to your partner's non-verbal signals can enhance emotional intimacy and understanding, fostering a stronger bond.

In conclusion, both verbal and non-verbal communication are integral to effective interaction. While verbal communication allows for the conveyance of detailed and complex information, non-verbal communication enriches and adds depth to these messages by expressing emotions and attitudes. The key to successful communication lies in the harmonious integration of both forms, paying attention to the alignment between what is said and how it is said. By honing skills in both areas, one can navigate personal and professional interactions with greater clarity, empathy, and effectiveness. Whether you are leading a team, resolving a conflict, or simply connecting with a friend, the ability to communicate effectively using both words and actions is a powerful tool in fostering understanding and building meaningful relationships. Understanding the nuances of verbal and non-verbal communication also requires an awareness of the context in which the communication occurs. Context shapes how messages are constructed, delivered, and interpreted. For example, a casual conversation with a friend at a coffee shop provides a relaxed environment where informal language and playful gestures are appropriate. In contrast, a formal business meeting demands a more structured approach, with precise language and controlled body movements to maintain professionalism.

The Role of Emotions in Communication

Emotions are the lifeblood of human communication, infusing our interactions with depth, meaning, and nuance. Whether we are aware of it or not, emotions influence how we perceive messages, how we convey our thoughts, and how others respond to us. Understanding the role of emotions in communication is essential for building meaningful relationships, resolving conflicts, and effectively conveying our intentions.

Imagine a scenario where two colleagues are discussing a project deadline. One colleague, stressed and anxious, might communicate their concerns with a sharp tone and hurried speech. The other, more relaxed and confident, might respond with calm reassurances and a steady voice. Even though both are discussing the same topic, their emotional states significantly affect how their messages are delivered and received. The anxious colleague's emotions could heighten the sense of urgency, while the calm colleague's demeanor might help to soothe and reassure.

Emotions act as a filter through which we process information and experiences. When we feel positive emotions like happiness or excitement, we are more likely to approach communication with openness and enthusiasm. Conversely, negative emotions such as anger, fear, or sadness can lead to defensive, aggressive, or withdrawn communication styles. These emotional filters shape our interpretations and reactions, making it crucial to be aware of our emotional state and its potential impact on our interactions.

One of the key aspects of emotional communication is empathy—the ability to understand and share the feelings of another person. Empathy allows us to connect with others on a deeper level, fostering trust and cooperation. When we empathize with someone, we are better equipped to respond to their emotional needs and concerns. For example, if a friend is upset, acknowledging their feelings and offering supportive words can help them feel understood and valued, strengthening the bond between you.

Emotional intelligence, the capacity to recognize, understand, and manage our own emotions and those of others, plays a vital role in effective communication. Individuals with high emotional intelligence are adept at navigating the emotional landscapes of their interactions. They can accurately read emotional cues, regulate their own emotional responses, and influence the emotional states of others positively. This skill set is particularly important in leadership roles, where the ability to inspire and motivate often hinges on emotional resonance.

Consider a leader delivering a speech to their team. A leader with high emotional intelligence will not only convey the necessary information but will also engage the team emotionally. They might share a personal story that resonates with the team's experiences, use an enthusiastic tone to generate excitement, and maintain eye contact to establish connection. By doing so, they create an emotional atmosphere that motivates and unites the team.

Conflict is an inevitable part of human interaction, and emotions often run high in these situations. Effective conflict resolution requires acknowledging and addressing the emotional dimensions of the conflict. Ignoring emotions can lead to misunderstandings and unresolved tensions. For instance, in a disagreement between colleagues, it is important to recognize not just the factual basis of the conflict but also the emotions involved. Addressing these emotions through active listening, validation, and empathy can pave the way for a more constructive resolution.

Non-verbal communication is a powerful vehicle for expressing emotions. Facial expressions, gestures, posture, and tone of voice all convey emotional information, often more powerfully than words alone. A smile can communicate warmth and friendliness, while crossed arms might signal defensiveness or discomfort. Being attuned to these non-verbal cues can enhance our ability to interpret and respond to the emotional states of others. For example, noticing a colleague's tense posture during a meeting might prompt you to address their concerns more sensitively.

In romantic relationships, emotions play a central role in communication. Expressions of love, affection, frustration, and disappointment all shape the dynamics of the relationship. Emotional honesty is key to building and maintaining intimacy. Partners who can openly share their feelings and listen to each other's emotional needs are more likely to build a strong, resilient bond. For instance, expressing gratitude and appreciation regularly can reinforce positive feelings and deepen the connection between partners.

Emotions also influence our persuasive abilities. When trying to persuade someone, appealing to their emotions can be more effective than relying solely on logical arguments. Storytelling is a powerful tool in this regard. By sharing a compelling story that evokes emotions, you can create a connection with your audience and make your message more memorable. For example, a charity organization might share the personal stories of individuals they have helped, eliciting empathy and motivating potential donors to contribute.

In the workplace, emotions can impact productivity, collaboration, and overall job satisfaction. A positive emotional climate, where employees feel valued, supported, and motivated, can enhance performance and foster a collaborative spirit. Managers play a crucial role in cultivating this emotional climate. Recognizing and celebrating achievements, providing constructive feedback, and showing genuine concern for employees' well-being can contribute to a positive work environment. Conversely, a negative emotional climate, characterized by stress, fear, and dissatisfaction, can lead to disengagement and high turnover rates.

The digital age has introduced new challenges and opportunities for emotional communication. Text-based communication, such as emails and messages, lacks the non-verbal cues that convey emotions in face-to-face interactions. This can lead to misinterpretations and misunderstandings. To mitigate this, people often use emojis, punctuation, and formatting to convey tone and emotion. For instance, a smiley face can indicate friendliness, while exclamation marks can express excitement. Video calls and voice messages reintroduce some of the non-verbal elements, allowing for richer emotional expression.

Self-awareness is a cornerstone of effective emotional communication. Being aware of our own emotions and how they influence our communication helps us to manage our responses and interactions more effectively. Techniques such as mindfulness and reflection can enhance self-awareness. By regularly taking time to reflect on our emotional experiences and their impact on our communication, we can develop greater emotional insight and control.

In educational settings, emotions significantly affect learning and communication. Teachers who create an emotionally supportive classroom environment can enhance students' engagement and motivation. Positive reinforcement, encouragement, and a genuine interest in students' well-being contribute to a conducive learning atmosphere. Conversely, negative emotions such as anxiety or fear can hinder learning and communication. Understanding the emotional needs of students and addressing them thoughtfully can lead to more effective teaching and learning experiences.

In conclusion, emotions are integral to all forms of communication, shaping how we convey and interpret messages. By developing emotional intelligence, practicing empathy, and being mindful of both verbal and non-verbal emotional cues, we can enhance our communication skills and build stronger, more meaningful connections with others. Whether in personal relationships, professional environments, or digital interactions, the ability to navigate the emotional dimensions of communication is a powerful tool for achieving clarity, understanding, and harmony. Emotions also play a pivotal role in cultural communication. Different cultures have varying norms and expectations regarding the expression and interpretation of emotions. For example, in some cultures, openly displaying emotions such as joy or sadness is common and accepted, while in others, such displays might be seen as inappropriate or a sign of weakness. Understanding and respecting these cultural differences is crucial for effective cross-cultural communication.

Common Barriers to Effective Communication

Effective communication is pivotal to human interaction, yet numerous barriers can impede its success. Understanding these obstacles is essential for anyone striving to improve their communication skills. These barriers can arise from a variety of sources, including personal biases, environmental distractions, and cultural differences. By identifying and addressing these common barriers, individuals can enhance their ability to convey messages clearly and understand others more accurately.

One of the most pervasive barriers to effective communication is language. Even when speakers share a common language, differences in dialects, jargon, and slang can create misunderstandings. Consider a scenario where a medical professional uses technical jargon to explain a diagnosis to a patient. The patient might nod along, not wanting to appear uninformed, yet leave the conversation without a clear understanding of their condition. To overcome this barrier, it is crucial to tailor language to the audience's level of understanding, avoiding unnecessary complexity and checking for comprehension frequently.

Cultural differences present another significant barrier. Culture shapes how we interpret messages and express ourselves. For example, in some cultures, direct eye contact is a sign of confidence and honesty, while in others, it can be perceived as aggressive or disrespectful. Misinterpretations stemming from cultural norms can lead to confusion and conflict. To mitigate this, developing cultural competence and being mindful of different communication styles can foster more effective interactions. This involves not only learning about other cultures but also reflecting on one's own communication practices and how they might be perceived by others.

Emotional barriers are also prevalent in communication. Strong emotions such as anger, fear, or frustration can cloud judgment and hinder the ability to communicate effectively. Imagine a heated argument where both parties are too focused on their own emotions to listen to each other. In such cases, taking a step back to manage emotions before continuing the conversation can lead to more productive outcomes. Techniques such as deep breathing, taking a break, or even writing down thoughts can help in regulating emotions and facilitating clearer communication.

Physical barriers, such as noise and distance, can also disrupt communication. In a noisy environment, it can be challenging to hear and understand the speaker, leading to frustration and errors. Similarly, physical distance, especially in the context of remote communication, can make it difficult to pick up on non-verbal cues like body language and facial expressions. To address these barriers, ensuring a quiet environment for conversations and using technology to bridge physical gaps—such as video calls for remote discussions—can enhance the clarity of communication.

Perceptual barriers occur when individuals have different interpretations of the same message. These differences can stem from personal experiences, beliefs, and biases. For instance, two employees might perceive feedback from their manager differently: one might see it as constructive criticism, while the other perceives it as an attack. Being aware of these perceptual differences and striving for clarity in messaging can help reduce misunderstandings. Asking for feedback on how a message was received and clarifying any ambiguities can also be beneficial.

Listening barriers are perhaps the most underestimated yet crucial obstacles in communication. Effective communication is a two-way process that requires active listening, not just speaking. However, many people listen with the intent to reply rather than to understand. This can lead to missed information and misinterpretations.

Practicing active listening—paying full attention, avoiding interruptions, and reflecting back what you heard—can greatly enhance communication effectiveness. For instance, during a team meeting, summarizing key points discussed and asking for confirmation ensures that everyone is on the same page.

Psychological barriers, such as stress and anxiety, can impair one's ability to communicate effectively. Stress can lead to hurried, unclear communication, while anxiety might cause an individual to withdraw and avoid interaction altogether. Recognizing these barriers and addressing the underlying causes, such as by practicing stress management techniques or seeking professional support, can improve communication. For example, a student anxious about a presentation might benefit from rehearsal and relaxation techniques to boost confidence and clarity.

Stereotyping and prejudice are significant barriers that can distort communication. Preconceived notions about a person based on their background, appearance, or beliefs can lead to biased interpretations of their messages. This can create a barrier to genuine understanding and collaboration. Challenging these biases by actively seeking to understand the individual's perspective and experiences can help break down these barriers. For example, in a multicultural team, encouraging open dialogue about different viewpoints can promote inclusivity and better communication.

Technological barriers have become increasingly relevant in the digital age. While technology facilitates communication across distances, it also introduces challenges such as technical glitches, lack of personal touch, and information overload. A poorly timed software update or a malfunctioning microphone can derail a virtual meeting. To mitigate these barriers, being proficient with communication tools and having backup plans in place can ensure smoother interactions. Additionally, being mindful of the limitations of digital communication and supplementing it with personal interactions when possible can enhance effectiveness.

Semantic barriers arise from differences in understanding the meaning of words and phrases. Words can have multiple meanings, and without context, messages can be misinterpreted. For example, the word "issue" might be understood as a problem by one person but as a topic for discussion by another. To overcome semantic barriers, providing clear definitions and context can help ensure that the intended message is conveyed accurately. Using examples and analogies can also clarify complex ideas.

Organizational barriers, such as hierarchical structures and rigid protocols, can hinder open communication within an organization. Employees might be reluctant to share ideas or feedback due to fear of repercussions or a belief that their input won't be valued. Creating an open and inclusive communication culture, where feedback is encouraged and valued at all levels, can help break down these barriers. For instance, regular town hall meetings and anonymous feedback channels can provide platforms for open communication.

Barriers related to differences in communication styles can also impact effectiveness. Some people prefer direct, concise communication, while others might use a more indirect, elaborate style. Misalignment in communication styles can lead to frustration and misunderstandings. Acknowledging these differences and adapting one's style to the audience can enhance communication. For example, in a multicultural team, being flexible and accommodating different communication preferences can foster better collaboration.

In conclusion, effective communication is often hindered by a range of barriers, from language and cultural differences to emotional and psychological obstacles. By recognizing and addressing these barriers, individuals can enhance their communication skills and foster more meaningful, accurate, and productive interactions. Whether in personal relationships, professional settings, or cross-cultural exchanges, the ability to navigate these barriers is essential for achieving clarity, understanding, and connection. Through continuous learning and adaptation, we can overcome these challenges and improve our overall communication effectiveness. Navigating these barriers requires a proactive approach and a willingness to adapt. Strategies for overcoming communication barriers can be implemented on both personal and organizational levels, ensuring that messages are transmitted and received as intended.

Improving Listening Skills

Listening is an indispensable component of effective communication, yet it is often underappreciated and underdeveloped. Mastering the art of listening can transform personal and professional relationships, fostering deeper understanding and reducing conflicts. Improving listening skills involves more than just hearing words; it requires active engagement, empathy, and a conscious effort to understand the speaker's message fully.

Consider a busy executive juggling multiple tasks while meeting with a team member. The executive may hear the team member's words but miss the underlying concerns or ideas due to distractions. True listening demands focus and the ability to tune out external and internal noise to fully engage with the speaker.

One practical approach to improving listening skills is to cultivate active listening. Active listening involves fully concentrating on the speaker, understanding their message, responding thoughtfully, and remembering what was said. It is a dynamic process that requires the listener's full attention and engagement. Techniques for active listening include maintaining eye contact, nodding to show understanding, and providing feedback through paraphrasing or summarizing the speaker's points. For instance, if a colleague explains a complex project, an active listener might respond with, "So, what you're saying is that we need to prioritize task A before moving on to task B, correct?"

Empathy plays a crucial role in listening. By putting oneself in the speaker's shoes, a listener can better understand the emotions and motivations behind the words. This empathetic approach can bridge gaps in communication and foster a more supportive environment. For example, when a friend shares a personal struggle, an empathetic listener might say, "I can see how that would be really challenging for you. I'm here to support you." This kind of response not only validates the speaker's feelings but also strengthens the bond between the individuals.

Eliminating distractions is essential for effective listening. In today's digital age, it is easy to become distracted by smartphones, emails, or social media. These distractions can prevent a listener from fully engaging with the speaker. Setting aside dedicated time for conversations, turning off electronic devices, and choosing a quiet environment can significantly enhance listening. Imagine a scenario where a manager meets with an employee to discuss performance feedback. By choosing a private office and silencing their phone, the manager can ensure that the employee feels heard and valued.

Listening also involves being aware of non-verbal cues. Body language, facial expressions, and tone of voice can convey much more than words alone. By paying attention to these non-verbal signals, a listener can gain a deeper understanding of the speaker's message. For instance, if a team member says they are "fine" but their body language suggests otherwise, an attentive listener might gently probe further to uncover any underlying issues. This attentiveness can prevent misunderstandings and address concerns before they escalate.

Asking open-ended questions is another effective strategy for improving listening skills. Open-ended questions encourage the speaker to elaborate and provide more detailed information, fostering a richer dialogue. Instead of asking yes-or-no questions, a listener might ask, "Can you tell me more about your experience with this project?" or "What challenges have you encountered, and how did you overcome them?" These questions signal genuine interest and encourage the speaker to share more, leading to a more meaningful conversation.

Reflective listening is a technique that involves mirroring the speaker's message to confirm understanding. This can be done by paraphrasing or summarizing what the speaker has said and then seeking confirmation. For example, if a team member expresses frustration about a tight deadline, a reflective listener might respond with, "It sounds like you're feeling overwhelmed by the deadline. Is that correct?" This technique ensures that the listener accurately understands the speaker's message and provides an opportunity for clarification if needed.

Being patient and avoiding interruptions are also critical aspects of effective listening. Interrupting a speaker can disrupt their train of thought and signal that their message is not valued. Allowing the speaker to finish their thoughts before responding shows respect and encourages a more open exchange. For instance, during a brainstorming session, allowing each team member to voice their ideas without interruption can lead to more innovative solutions and a more inclusive environment.

Developing listening skills also involves being mindful of one's biases and preconceptions. These can color how a listener interprets a message and lead to misunderstandings. By approaching each conversation with an open mind and a willingness to understand the speaker's perspective, a listener can overcome these biases and engage more fully. For example, in a multicultural team, being aware of and setting aside cultural preconceptions can foster a more respectful and productive dialogue.

Practicing mindfulness can enhance listening skills by helping individuals remain present and focused during conversations. Mindfulness involves paying attention to the current moment without judgment. By practicing mindfulness techniques, such as deep breathing or meditation, individuals can develop greater awareness and concentration, which can be applied to listening. For instance, before a crucial meeting, taking a few moments to breathe deeply and center oneself can improve focus and attentiveness during the conversation.

Feedback is a valuable tool for improving listening skills. Seeking feedback from others on one's listening abilities can provide insights into areas for improvement. For example, after a team meeting, a manager might ask team members for feedback on their listening skills, such as whether they felt heard and understood. This feedback can highlight strengths and identify areas where the manager can improve, leading to better communication and stronger relationships.

Improving listening skills is an ongoing process that requires practice and dedication. By incorporating these strategies into daily interactions, individuals can enhance their ability to listen effectively and build stronger, more meaningful connections. Whether in personal relationships, professional settings, or casual conversations, the ability to listen well is a powerful tool for fostering understanding, reducing conflicts, and achieving better outcomes.

Listening is not just about hearing words; it is about understanding the speaker's message, emotions, and intentions. By practicing active listening, showing empathy, eliminating distractions, being aware of non-verbal cues, asking open-ended questions, reflecting messages, being patient, recognizing biases, practicing mindfulness, and seeking feedback, individuals can significantly improve their listening skills. These efforts can lead to more effective communication, stronger relationships, and a deeper understanding of others.

In summary, improving listening skills is essential for effective communication and building stronger connections. It requires a conscious effort and the application of various techniques and strategies. By dedicating time and attention to developing these skills, individuals can enhance their ability to listen, understand, and respond to others, leading to more meaningful and productive interactions. Listening is a fundamental skill that extends beyond personal interactions; it is crucial in professional environments where teamwork, leadership, and client relations are paramount. Effective listening can be the difference between success and failure in these contexts, as it fosters a culture of openness, collaboration, and mutual respect.

Chapter 3

Building Trust through Communication

The Foundation of Trust

Trust forms the bedrock of all meaningful relationships, whether personal or professional. It is the invisible thread that connects individuals, enabling them to rely on each other, share vulnerabilities, and collaborate effectively. Building and maintaining trust is a complex process that requires consistent effort, integrity, and empathy.

Imagine a scenario where a new leader takes charge of a team that has experienced a series of management changes. The team's morale is low, and skepticism runs high. For the new leader, establishing trust is paramount. This can be achieved through transparent communication, demonstrating competence, and showing genuine concern for team members' well-being. By consistently following through on promises and being open about challenges and decisions, the leader can gradually earn the team's trust.

Transparency is a cornerstone of trust. When individuals are open and honest about their intentions, actions, and decisions, it fosters an environment where others feel safe to do the same. In a professional setting, this might involve sharing the rationale behind strategic decisions, openly discussing challenges and setbacks, and being forthright about one's limitations. For example, a project manager facing a tight deadline might openly communicate the constraints to the team and collaboratively seek solutions, rather than masking the difficulties and risking a last-minute crisis.

Consistency is equally crucial. People tend to trust those who are reliable and predictable in their actions. This means adhering to the commitments one makes, whether they are as significant as delivering a major project on time or as minor as attending a scheduled meeting. Consistency in behavior builds a reputation of dependability, which is a key ingredient in the trust-building process. Consider a colleague who consistently meets their deadlines and delivers high-quality work; over time, you come to rely on them and trust their capabilities and dedication.

Empathy and active listening are vital in cultivating trust. When individuals feel heard and understood, it creates a sense of connection and validation. In a personal relationship, this might mean taking the time to listen to a partner's concerns without interrupting or judging, demonstrating that their feelings and perspectives matter. In a workplace, a manager who listens to employees' ideas and feedback, and acts upon them when appropriate, shows respect and values their contributions. This practice not only builds trust but also enhances engagement and collaboration.

Trust is also built through vulnerability. Sharing one's own challenges, mistakes, and uncertainties can humanize an individual and make them more relatable. This openness can encourage others to do the same, fostering a culture of mutual support and understanding. For instance, a leader who admits to a mistake and discusses what they have learned from it can inspire their team to view setbacks as learning opportunities rather than failures to be hidden.

Respecting confidentiality is another critical aspect of trust. When people share sensitive information, they need to be confident that it will not be disclosed without their consent. Breaching this trust can cause irreparable damage to relationships. In a professional context, maintaining confidentiality might involve safeguarding client information or not sharing a colleague's personal issues with others. Trust is fragile, and once broken, it can be challenging to rebuild.

Mutual respect is foundational to trust. Treating others with dignity, valuing their opinions, and recognizing their contributions creates an environment where trust can flourish. This respect should be evident in everyday interactions, from acknowledging a team member's hard work to considering their input in decision-making processes. For example, in a collaborative project, ensuring that all voices are heard and credited can build a strong, trust-based team dynamic.

Building trust also involves demonstrating integrity. Acting ethically and aligning one's actions with their values and principles is essential. When individuals see that someone consistently does the right thing, even when it is difficult, it reinforces their confidence in that person's character. Imagine a situation where a company faces a financial shortfall. A leader who chooses to be honest about the situation, rather than concealing it, and works transparently with the team to find solutions, exemplifies integrity and strengthens trust.

Trust is not static; it requires ongoing nurturing and reinforcement. Regular check-ins, open communication, and a willingness to address and resolve conflicts are all part of maintaining trust. This continuous effort ensures that trust remains strong and can withstand challenges. For instance, in a long-term partnership, regular conversations about expectations, concerns, and aspirations can help both parties stay aligned and address any issues before they become significant problems.

Rebuilding trust after it has been broken is particularly challenging but not impossible. It requires acknowledgment of the breach, a sincere apology, and consistent efforts to demonstrate changed behavior over time. Rebuilding trust is a gradual process that demands patience and perseverance. For example, if a leader loses their team's trust due to a failure to deliver on promises, they must openly acknowledge the failure, apologize, and then take concrete steps to rebuild credibility through consistent and transparent actions.

Trust is also closely linked to accountability. Holding oneself and others accountable for their actions reinforces a culture of trust. This means not only taking responsibility for one's successes but also for mistakes and failures. In a team setting, this might involve regular reviews where team members discuss what went well and what could be improved, fostering a culture of continuous improvement and mutual accountability.

In summary, trust is the foundation upon which strong, effective relationships are built. It requires transparency, consistency, empathy, vulnerability, and respect for confidentiality, mutual respect, integrity, ongoing effort, and accountability. Whether in personal relationships or professional environments, cultivating trust leads to deeper connections, better collaboration, and more successful outcomes. By making a conscious effort to build and maintain trust, individuals and organizations can create environments where people feel valued, understood, and empowered to contribute their best. Trust is also a powerful motivator. When individuals feel trusted, they are more likely to take ownership of their responsibilities and go above and beyond in their efforts. This sense of ownership and responsibility can drive innovation and productivity. For instance, employees who feel trusted by their managers are often more willing to take initiative, propose new ideas, and take calculated risks, knowing that their efforts are supported and valued.

Open and Honest Conversations

Open and honest conversations are the lifeblood of any thriving relationship, whether personal, professional, or communal. These dialogues foster mutual understanding, build deeper connections, and pave the way for resolving conflicts and creating shared visions. Embracing open and honest communication requires courage, empathy, and the willingness to be vulnerable.

Consider a family dinner where everyone is encouraged to share their thoughts and feelings about a recent move to a new city. By creating a safe space for each family member to express their concerns and hopes, the family can collectively navigate the transition more smoothly. The children might voice their fears about making new friends, while the parents can share their excitement about new opportunities. This kind of open dialogue ensures that everyone's perspective is valued, reducing anxiety and fostering a sense of unity.

In the workplace, open and honest conversations are crucial for team dynamics and organizational growth. Imagine a project team facing delays due to unforeseen challenges. Instead of assigning blame or hiding the issues, team members are encouraged to discuss the problems openly. This transparency allows the team to brainstorm solutions collectively and distribute the workload more effectively. A culture of open communication can significantly reduce misunderstandings and enhance collaboration.

Active listening is a fundamental component of open and honest conversations. It involves fully concentrating, understanding, responding, and remembering what is being said. When someone feels genuinely heard, they are more likely to open up and engage in meaningful dialogue. For instance, a manager who listens attentively to an employee's feedback about a new process shows that they value the employee's input, fostering a sense of trust and respect.

Empathy plays a vital role in these conversations. It involves putting oneself in the other person's shoes and understanding their emotions and perspectives. Consider a scenario where a friend confides about a personal struggle. Responding with empathy— acknowledging their feelings and offering support— strengthens the bond between friends and encourages continued openness. In professional settings, empathetic leaders who understand and address their team's concerns can build a more motivated and loyal workforce.

Honesty, while sometimes uncomfortable, is essential in maintaining the integrity of conversations. It requires speaking the truth even when it might be difficult or unpopular. For example, a team leader might need to provide constructive feedback to an underperforming team member. Delivering this feedback honestly, yet tactfully, can help the team member improve and feel respected. Honest communication prevents the buildup of unresolved issues and promotes a culture of transparency.

The timing and context of conversations matter significantly. Choosing the right moment and setting can impact the effectiveness of the dialogue. Discussing sensitive topics in a private and relaxed environment, rather than in a hurried or public setting, can lead to more productive and positive outcomes. For instance, addressing a colleague's recurring tardiness in a private meeting room after work hours is more respectful and effective than confronting them in front of the team during a busy day.

Non-verbal communication also plays a crucial role in open and honest conversations. Body language, facial expressions, and tone of voice can all convey sincerity, openness, and respect. Maintaining eye contact, nodding in acknowledgment, and using a calm and steady tone can enhance the message being communicated and reinforce the speaker's intent. For example, a teacher addressing a student's concern with a warm smile and attentive posture reassures the student that their issue is being taken seriously.

Conflict resolution is another area where open and honest conversations are indispensable. When conflicts arise, addressing them head-on with transparency and a willingness to understand all sides can prevent escalation and lead to mutually beneficial solutions. Consider two business partners who have differing visions for their company's future. By engaging in a candid discussion, where both parties openly share their ideas and concerns, they can find common ground and devise a strategy that aligns with both of their goals.

Building the habit of open and honest communication requires practice and commitment. It involves being mindful of one's own communication style and actively working to improve it. For example, someone who tends to avoid confrontation might practice addressing minor issues directly and respectfully, gradually building confidence for more significant conversations. Similarly, someone who is overly blunt might work on softening their approach to ensure their honesty doesn't come across as harsh.

Feedback is a powerful tool in fostering open and honest conversations. Both giving and receiving feedback constructively can promote growth and improvement. When giving feedback, it is essential to focus on specific behaviors rather than personal attributes, use "I" statements to express how the behavior affects you, and offer suggestions for improvement. When receiving feedback, listening without interrupting, asking clarifying questions, and reflecting on the feedback can lead to personal and professional development. For instance, a colleague providing feedback might say, "I noticed the report was submitted late, which impacted our timeline. Could we discuss ways to ensure timely submissions in the future?"

Creating a culture of open and honest communication within an organization or community involves setting clear expectations and leading by example. Leaders and key members must model the behavior they wish to see, demonstrating openness, honesty, and respect in their interactions. Regularly scheduled meetings or forums where individuals can voice their thoughts and concerns without fear of judgment or reprisal can institutionalize this culture. For example, a company might implement monthly town hall meetings where employees are encouraged to share their ideas and feedback with senior management.

Trust is the foundation upon which open and honest conversations are built. When people trust that their words will be met with respect and consideration, they are more likely to engage in open dialogue. This trust is cultivated through consistent, respectful, and empathetic communication over time. For instance, a mentor who consistently provides constructive feedback and support to their mentee builds a trusting relationship, encouraging the mentee to be more open about their challenges and aspirations.

In summary, open and honest conversations are essential for building and maintaining healthy relationships across all areas of life. They require active listening, empathy, honesty, appropriate timing, effective non-verbal communication, and a commitment to continuous improvement. By fostering a culture of open communication, individuals and organizations can create environments where trust, collaboration, and growth thrive. Trust is not built overnight; it requires a consistent demonstration of integrity and respect. In everyday interactions, small gestures like acknowledging someone's effort, maintaining confidentiality, and following through on promises contribute to a foundation of trust. For example, if a colleague confides in you about a personal issue, respecting their privacy and offering support can strengthen your relationship and encourage further open communication.

Handling Secrets and Privacy

Secrets and privacy form the intricate fabric of human relationships, weaving through personal, professional, and societal interactions. Navigating this delicate terrain requires a nuanced understanding of when to safeguard information and when to disclose it, balancing the need for transparency with the imperative of confidentiality.

Consider the story of Sarah, a manager at a midsize company. Sarah prided herself on creating an open and honest work environment. However, she also understood that certain information needed to be kept

confidential for the well-being of her team and the
organization. When an employee confided in her
about a personal health issue, Sarah faced a dilemma.
She needed to respect the employee's privacy while
also considering the broader implications for the
team's workload and project timelines. By
maintaining the confidentiality of the employee's
health issue and working discreetly to adjust project
plans, Sarah was able to honor the individual's privacy
while ensuring the team's success.

Privacy is a fundamental human right, vital for
personal autonomy and dignity. It allows individuals
to control the flow of their personal information,
safeguarding them from undue scrutiny and potential
harm. In the digital age, privacy has become even
more critical as vast amounts of personal data are
collected and stored online. Understanding and
managing privacy involves recognizing the value of
personal information and learning how to protect it.

Secrets, on the other hand, are pieces of information
deliberately kept hidden from others. While not
inherently negative, secrets can range from harmless
to potentially damaging. The key lies in discerning the
nature of the secret and the potential consequences of
its disclosure or concealment. For example, a surprise
birthday party is a type of secret intended to bring joy,
while withholding information about a company's
impending layoffs can lead to mistrust and anxiety
among employees.

Trust is the cornerstone of handling secrets and
privacy effectively. When someone entrusts you with
their personal information or a secret, they are
placing their confidence in your discretion and

integrity. Betraying this trust can have severe repercussions, damaging relationships and reputations. For instance, if a friend shares a personal struggle with you in confidence, revealing that information to others without their consent would breach their trust and likely harm your friendship.

In professional settings, maintaining confidentiality is often a legal and ethical obligation. Many industries, such as healthcare, law, and finance, have strict regulations governing the handling of sensitive information. Breaching these regulations can result in legal penalties and loss of professional credibility. For example, a lawyer who discloses a client's confidential information without authorization could face disbarment and legal action.

Creating a culture of respect for privacy and confidentiality within an organization involves clear policies and consistent practices. Employees should be educated about the importance of protecting sensitive information and the protocols for handling it. Regular training sessions and reminders can reinforce these principles, ensuring that everyone understands their responsibilities. For instance, a company might implement mandatory annual training on data privacy and cybersecurity to keep employees informed about best practices and emerging threats.

In personal relationships, the decision to keep or share a secret can be complex. It often requires balancing loyalty to the person who confided in you with your own ethical standards and the potential impact on others. For example, if you discover that a close friend is engaging in harmful behavior, you might struggle with whether to keep their secret or intervene to prevent further harm. In such cases, seeking guidance from a trusted mentor or professional can help you navigate the ethical dilemmas involved.

The digital age has introduced new challenges to handling secrets and privacy. Social media, cloud storage, and other technologies have made it easier to share information but also more difficult to control its dissemination. Understanding digital privacy involves being aware of how your data is collected, used, and shared. It also means taking proactive steps to protect your information, such as using strong passwords, enabling two-factor authentication, and being cautious about what you share online.

For instance, consider the case of Jessica, who frequently posted updates about her life on social media. One day, she shared details about an upcoming vacation, including the dates she would be away. Unbeknownst to her, a potential burglar saw the post and targeted her home while she was gone. This experience taught Jessica the importance of being mindful about the information she shared online and the potential risks to her privacy and security.

Handling secrets and privacy often involves ethical considerations. Ethical decision-making requires a thoughtful analysis of the potential consequences of sharing or withholding information. It involves considering the rights and well-being of all parties affected by the decision. For example, a journalist who uncovers a government scandal must weigh the public's right to know against the potential harm that disclosing the information might cause to individuals involved.

In families, privacy and secrets can significantly impact dynamics and relationships. Parents, for example, must balance their children's right to privacy with their responsibility to protect and guide them. This can be particularly challenging during adolescence when the need for independence and privacy becomes more pronounced. Open communication and mutual respect are essential for navigating these challenges. For instance, a parent who respects their teenager's privacy by knocking before entering their room demonstrates trust and respect, which can strengthen their relationship.

In friendships, the sharing and keeping of secrets can test the strength of the bond. A friend who consistently honors your confidence and respects your privacy is likely to be viewed as trustworthy and reliable. However, if a friend repeatedly breaks your trust by sharing your secrets, it can lead to feelings of betrayal and a weakening of the relationship. Understanding and respecting each other's boundaries is crucial for maintaining healthy and supportive friendships.

Privacy and secrets also play a significant role in romantic relationships. Partners must navigate the delicate balance between intimacy and personal boundaries. While sharing personal thoughts and experiences can deepen the connection, respecting each other's privacy is equally important. For example, partners who respect each other's need for personal space and autonomy are likely to build a stronger and more resilient relationship.

In summary, handling secrets and privacy involves a complex interplay of trust, ethics, and respect. Whether in personal relationships, professional settings, or the digital realm, the principles of discretion and confidentiality are essential for maintaining trust and protecting individual rights. By fostering a culture of respect for privacy and confidentiality, we can build stronger, more trustworthy relationships and create environments where everyone feels safe and valued. In addition to trust, ethics, and respect, transparency plays an important role in managing secrets and privacy effectively. Transparency doesn't mean revealing all details indiscriminately but rather communicating openly about how information is handled, who has access to it, and under what circumstances it might be shared. For instance, companies that clearly outline their privacy policies and data handling practices foster greater trust among their customers.

Rebuilding Trust after a Breach

Rebuilding trust after a breach is a nuanced and often daunting process. Trust, once broken, is not easily mended, but with concerted effort, transparency, and time, it can be restored. The journey to regain trust involves understanding the depth of the damage, sincere apologies, consistent actions, and open communication.

Consider the story of Alex and Maria, business partners who had built a successful startup from scratch. They trusted each other implicitly, dividing responsibilities and sharing the highs and lows of their entrepreneurial journey. However, Alex made a series of financial decisions without consulting Maria, leading to significant losses. When Maria discovered the unilateral actions, she felt betrayed and contemplated dissolving the partnership. Understanding the gravity of his mistake, Alex knew he had to take immediate steps to rebuild Maria's trust.

The first step in rebuilding trust is acknowledging the breach and understanding its impact. This involves a deep, honest reflection on what went wrong and how it affected the other party. For Alex, this meant recognizing that his actions had not only jeopardized their business but also violated the foundational trust in their relationship. He realized that regaining Maria's trust required more than just an apology; it needed a profound change in behavior and a commitment to transparency.

Apologizing sincerely is crucial. A genuine apology goes beyond simply saying "I'm sorry." It involves expressing regret, taking responsibility, and outlining steps to prevent a recurrence. When Alex approached Maria, he didn't just apologize for the financial loss. He acknowledged the breach of trust, explained his thought process, and admitted that his decisions were misguided. He expressed his commitment to making amends and asked Maria for the opportunity to prove himself.

Consistency in actions is essential to rebuilding trust. Words alone are insufficient; they must be backed by consistent and trustworthy behavior over time. Alex understood that regaining Maria's trust would require a sustained effort. He began by involving her in every decision, no matter how small, and sought her input regularly. This shift toward greater transparency and collaboration demonstrated his commitment to change.

Open communication plays a pivotal role in restoring trust. Keeping the lines of communication open helps address concerns, clarify misunderstandings, and rebuild a sense of security. Alex and Maria started having regular check-ins to discuss their business and any issues that arose. These conversations helped both of them feel heard and valued, gradually restoring the lost trust.

Patience is another critical element. Rebuilding trust is a gradual process and cannot be rushed. It requires patience from both parties—the one seeking forgiveness and the one granting it. Maria needed time to process her feelings and observe Alex's changed behavior. Alex, on the other hand, had to be patient and consistent, understanding that trust would not be restored overnight.

Transparency is vital in this process. Being open about one's actions and decisions helps rebuild credibility. For Alex, this meant being completely transparent about the company's finances and decision-making processes. He shared financial reports, invited Maria to meetings with stakeholders, and made sure she was fully informed about the business's status. This level of openness reassured Maria and helped rebuild her trust.

A supportive environment can also facilitate the rebuilding of trust. Surrounding oneself with supportive friends, family, or colleagues can provide the necessary strength and encouragement. Maria sought advice from trusted friends and mentors, who helped her understand Alex's perspective and the efforts he was making to rebuild trust. Their support played a crucial role in her decision to give Alex another chance.

Forgiveness is an integral part of rebuilding trust. It involves letting go of resentment and bitterness, which can be a challenging process. Maria's decision to forgive Alex was not easy, but she realized that holding onto anger would only harm their partnership and her own peace of mind. Forgiveness allowed her to move forward and give Alex the opportunity to prove himself.

Personal growth often accompanies the process of rebuilding trust. Both parties can learn valuable lessons and emerge stronger from the experience. Alex's breach of trust taught him the importance of collaboration and transparency. For Maria, the experience highlighted the significance of clear communication and setting boundaries. These lessons not only helped them rebuild their partnership but also strengthened their individual characters.

In addition to personal relationships, rebuilding trust is equally crucial in professional settings. Consider the case of a company that suffers a data breach, compromising customers' personal information. The company must take immediate steps to address the breach, communicate transparently with affected customers, and implement measures to prevent future incidents. This might involve enhancing security protocols, offering credit monitoring services, and being open about the steps taken to rectify the situation. By demonstrating a commitment to protecting customer data and being transparent about their efforts, the company can gradually rebuild customer trust.

In communities, rebuilding trust can be a collective effort. When a community faces a breach of trust, such as a local government scandal, the rebuilding process involves not only the individuals directly involved but also the entire community. Transparent investigations, public apologies, and reforms can help restore faith in local institutions. Community leaders must engage in open dialogues with residents, address their concerns, and involve them in decision-making processes to rebuild trust.

Rebuilding trust after a breach is a complex and multifaceted process. It requires a combination of sincere apologies, consistent actions, open communication, patience, transparency, support, forgiveness, and personal growth. Whether in personal relationships, professional settings, or communities, the principles of honesty, accountability, and empathy are essential for restoring trust. By understanding the depth of the breach, committing to change, and demonstrating trustworthy behavior over time, it is possible to rebuild and even strengthen the bonds of trust. As Alex and Maria continued their journey of rebuilding trust, they discovered a few more strategies that helped solidify their renewed partnership. They realized that celebrating small victories and progress could be incredibly motivating. Each time Maria noticed Alex consistently involving her in decision-making, she acknowledged it, which reinforced Alex's commitment to transparency. This positive reinforcement created a virtuous cycle, encouraging both to maintain the new patterns of behavior.

Trust-Building Activities for Couples

Trust-building activities for couples can significantly enhance the bond and intimacy between partners. These activities are designed to foster open communication, mutual understanding, and shared experiences, which are essential components of a healthy and trusting relationship. By engaging in various trust-building exercises, couples can strengthen their connection and create a solid foundation for their relationship.

One effective trust-building activity is practicing active listening. This involves giving your partner your full attention when they are speaking, without interrupting or thinking about your response. Active listening shows respect and appreciation for your partner's thoughts and feelings. To practice this, set aside time each day to have a conversation where each person has the opportunity to speak while the other listens attentively. Reflect back what you hear to ensure understanding, and ask questions to deepen the conversation.

Another powerful activity is engaging in vulnerability exercises. Vulnerability is a cornerstone of trust, and sharing personal thoughts, fears, and dreams can bring partners closer together. One way to do this is through a "vulnerability jar," where each partner writes down something they feel vulnerable about on a piece of paper and places it in the jar. Once a week, draw a slip from the jar and discuss it openly, offering support and understanding to each other.

Physical touch and non-verbal communication also play a critical role in building trust. Activities such as holding hands, hugging, or even sitting close to each other can foster a sense of security and warmth. One specific exercise is the "mirroring" activity, where couples face each other and mirror each other's movements without speaking. This non-verbal communication can enhance empathy and understanding, reinforcing the emotional connection.

Shared experiences and adventures can create lasting memories and a sense of partnership. Planning and undertaking new activities together, such as hiking, cooking a new recipe, or traveling, can strengthen your bond. These experiences require cooperation, communication, and mutual support, all of which are vital for building trust. For example, cooking together can be both fun and educational, allowing you to work as a team, share responsibilities, and enjoy the fruits of your labor.

Setting and achieving goals together can also enhance trust. By working towards a common objective, couples can develop a sense of unity and purpose. Start by discussing your individual and shared goals, and then create a plan to achieve them. This could be anything from saving for a vacation to completing a home project. The key is to support each other and celebrate your successes along the way, reinforcing your partnership.

Practicing gratitude is another impactful trust-building activity. Regularly expressing appreciation for your partner can strengthen your emotional connection and reinforce positive behaviors. Consider keeping a "gratitude journal" where you write down things you appreciate about your partner each day. Share these entries with each other weekly, creating a positive feedback loop that enhances trust and affection.

Mindfulness and meditation can also play a significant role in building trust. These practices encourage present-moment awareness and emotional regulation, which can reduce misunderstandings and conflicts. Try meditating together, focusing on your breath and letting go of distractions. Guided meditations specifically designed for couples can help you connect on a deeper level and cultivate a sense of calm and harmony in your relationship.

Conflict resolution skills are crucial for maintaining trust, especially during disagreements. Learning to navigate conflicts healthily can prevent damage to your relationship and build resilience. One effective method is the "timeout" strategy, where couples agree to take a break during heated arguments to cool down and reflect before continuing the discussion. This approach helps prevent hurtful words and actions, allowing for more constructive and respectful communication.

Participating in trust-building games can also be beneficial. Games like "trust falls," where one partner falls backward, trusting the other to catch them, can physically and emotionally reinforce the concept of relying on each other. Other games, such as "truth or dare" with a focus on honesty and openness, can also facilitate deeper conversations and understanding.

Couples therapy or workshops can provide structured and guided trust-building activities. These sessions, led by professionals, offer tools and techniques tailored to your relationship's specific needs. Participating in therapy or workshops demonstrates a commitment to improving your relationship and can offer valuable insights and strategies.

Creating rituals and traditions together can foster a sense of stability and continuity in your relationship. Whether it's a weekly date night, a morning coffee ritual, or yearly vacation traditions, these shared routines can reinforce your bond and provide a sense of security. These rituals serve as reminders of your commitment to each other and create a shared history that strengthens your connection.

Engaging in volunteer work or community service together can also build trust. Working side by side in a meaningful cause promotes teamwork and shared values. It allows you to see each other in a different light, often revealing strengths and qualities that enhance mutual respect and admiration. Volunteering can provide a sense of purpose and fulfillment that extends into your relationship.

Reading and discussing books on relationships and personal growth can be another trust-building activity. Choose books that offer insights and advice on communication, intimacy, and trust. Discussing the content and applying the lessons to your relationship can foster growth and understanding. It provides a platform for open dialogue and continuous learning about each other and the dynamics of a healthy partnership.

Finally, practicing forgiveness is essential for trust-building. Holding onto past grievances can erode trust and create emotional distance. Learning to forgive and let go of past hurts can pave the way for healing and renewal. This doesn't mean ignoring or excusing harmful behavior but rather addressing it, understanding its impact, and choosing to move forward with a commitment to positive change.

In conclusion, trust-building activities for couples encompass a wide range of practices, from communication exercises and shared experiences to mindfulness and conflict resolution. By incorporating these activities into your relationship, you can create a deeper, more resilient bond built on mutual respect, understanding, and affection. Trust is not built overnight; it requires consistent effort, patience, and a genuine commitment to your partner's well-being. Engaging in these activities can help you navigate challenges, celebrate successes, and grow together, ultimately leading to a stronger and more fulfilling relationship. Trust-building activities require ongoing dedication and a willingness to invest time and energy into your relationship. One important aspect is creating a safe space for open and honest communication. This involves setting aside regular time to discuss your feelings, thoughts, and concerns without fear of judgment or criticism. A weekly check-in can be an effective way to ensure both partners feel heard and understood. During these check-ins, focus on active listening, empathy, and validating each other's experiences.

Chapter 4

Emotional Intelligence in Relationships

What is Emotional Intelligence?

Emotional intelligence (EI) refers to the ability to recognize, understand, manage, and effectively use emotions in ourselves and in our interactions with others. It encompasses self-awareness, self-regulation, motivation, empathy, and social skills, forming a crucial component for personal and professional success. The concept gained prominence through the work of Daniel Goleman, who highlighted its importance alongside traditional intelligence (IQ).

Self-awareness is the foundation of emotional intelligence. It involves being in tune with your own emotions, understanding what you are feeling and why, and recognizing how your emotions can affect your thoughts and behavior. Imagine Jane, a manager who recognizes her frustration after a difficult meeting. Instead of lashing out, she takes a moment to understand her feelings, which allows her to address the issue constructively. By being aware of her emotional state, Jane can navigate her interactions more effectively, avoiding unnecessary conflicts and fostering a positive work environment.

Self-regulation builds on self-awareness and is the ability to manage your emotions, especially in stressful situations. It entails controlling impulses, staying calm under pressure, and responding to challenges with a level-headed approach. Consider John, who faces a tight deadline at work. Instead of panicking or becoming overwhelmed, he practices deep breathing and breaks down the task into manageable steps. This not only helps him maintain composure but also enhances his productivity and problem-solving abilities. Self-regulation allows individuals to handle their emotions in a healthy way, preventing negative reactions and promoting resilience.

Motivation within the context of emotional intelligence goes beyond external rewards and focuses on internal drive and persistence. People with high emotional intelligence are often motivated by a deep-seated desire to achieve personal goals and maintain their standards of excellence. Take Maria, an athlete training for a marathon. Her motivation is fueled not just by the prospect of winning but by her passion for running and personal growth. This intrinsic motivation drives her to push through obstacles and maintain a positive outlook, even during challenging times. Such motivation is essential for setting and achieving long-term goals and maintaining a sense of purpose.

Empathy, another critical component of emotional intelligence, is the ability to understand and share the feelings of others. It involves putting yourself in someone else's shoes and responding with compassion and understanding. For example, consider Michael, a teacher who notices a student struggling with a personal issue. Instead of dismissing the behavior as disruptive, he takes the time to listen and offer support. By demonstrating empathy,

Michael builds trust and rapport, creating a safe and supportive learning environment. Empathy enhances our ability to connect with others on a deeper level, fostering meaningful relationships and collaboration.

Social skills, the final component of emotional intelligence, encompass a range of interpersonal abilities that enable effective communication and relationship management. These skills include active listening, conflict resolution, teamwork, and leadership. Imagine Lisa, a team leader who excels in bringing her team together. She listens to her team members' concerns, mediates conflicts fairly, and motivates them towards a common goal. Her strong social skills not only enhance team cohesion but also drive collective success. Mastering social skills allows individuals to navigate complex social dynamics, build strong networks, and inspire others.

Emotional intelligence is not static; it can be developed and strengthened over time. One effective way to enhance EI is through mindfulness practices. Mindfulness involves paying attention to the present moment without judgment, which can increase self-awareness and emotional regulation. Practicing mindfulness meditation, for instance, can help you become more attuned to your emotional states and reactions. By regularly engaging in mindfulness, you can develop a greater sense of calm and clarity, enabling you to respond to situations with thoughtful intention rather than impulsive reactions.

Another approach to building emotional intelligence is through reflective journaling. By writing about your daily experiences, thoughts, and emotions, you can gain insights into your emotional patterns and triggers. Reflective journaling encourages self-exploration and helps identify areas for personal growth. For instance, if you frequently find yourself feeling frustrated during meetings, journaling can help uncover the underlying reasons and guide you towards strategies for improvement. This practice fosters greater self-awareness and can lead to more effective emotional regulation and interpersonal interactions.

Seeking feedback from others is also a valuable tool for enhancing emotional intelligence. Constructive feedback can provide an outside perspective on your behavior and its impact on others. For example, asking a trusted colleague for feedback on how you handle stress can reveal blind spots and offer opportunities for growth. By being open to feedback, you demonstrate a willingness to improve and build stronger relationships. It also encourages a culture of transparency and mutual support, which can enhance overall emotional intelligence within a team or organization.

Developing empathy can be facilitated by actively engaging in perspective-taking exercises. These exercises involve imagining yourself in someone else's situation and considering their feelings and viewpoints. For instance, if you are in a disagreement with a coworker, take a moment to reflect on their perspective and what they might be experiencing. This practice can soften your response and lead to more compassionate and effective communication. Engaging in activities that expose you to diverse perspectives, such as volunteering or community involvement, can also broaden your understanding and empathy.

Building strong social skills requires practice and intentional effort. One strategy is to focus on active listening, which involves fully concentrating on the speaker, understanding their message, and responding thoughtfully. During conversations, make a conscious effort to listen without interrupting, and reflect back what you hear to ensure understanding. This practice can improve communication and strengthen relationships. Additionally, honing conflict resolution skills by learning to address disagreements calmly and constructively can prevent misunderstandings and foster a collaborative environment.

Emotional intelligence has significant implications for various aspects of life, including personal relationships, career success, and overall well-being. In personal relationships, high EI can lead to deeper connections, greater trust, and more effective communication. For instance, couples who practice emotional intelligence are better equipped to navigate conflicts and support each other's emotional needs, resulting in stronger and more fulfilling relationships.

In the workplace, emotional intelligence is a key differentiator for effective leadership and teamwork. Leaders with high EI are able to inspire and motivate their teams, navigate challenges with resilience, and create a positive organizational culture. Employees with strong emotional intelligence are better at managing stress, collaborating with colleagues, and adapting to change. This can lead to increased job satisfaction, higher performance, and reduced turnover.

Overall well-being is also closely linked to emotional intelligence. Individuals with high EI tend to have better mental health, as they are more adept at managing stress and emotions. They are also more likely to engage in healthy coping strategies and maintain positive relationships, which contribute to a sense of fulfillment and happiness.

In conclusion, emotional intelligence is a multifaceted and dynamic skill that plays a crucial role in personal and professional success. By developing self-awareness, self-regulation, motivation, empathy, and social skills, individuals can enhance their emotional intelligence and improve their interactions with others. Through mindfulness, reflective journaling, seeking feedback, perspective-taking, and practicing social skills, emotional intelligence can be cultivated and strengthened. Its impact on relationships, career, and well-being underscores the importance of investing in emotional intelligence for a more fulfilling and successful life. Understanding and developing emotional intelligence can transform your day-to-day experiences and interactions. It not only enhances your interpersonal relationships but also contributes significantly to your overall mental and emotional well-being. The journey of cultivating emotional intelligence is ongoing, requiring continuous self-reflection, learning, and practice.

Developing Self-Awareness

Self-awareness is the cornerstone of emotional intelligence and personal growth. It involves a deep understanding of your own emotions, strengths, weaknesses, values, and motivations. This chapter delves into the process of developing self-awareness, exploring practical methods and exercises to enhance this critical skill.

Imagine being in a meeting where a colleague's comment irritates you. Without self-awareness, you might react impulsively, perhaps with frustration or defensiveness, escalating the situation unnecessarily. However, with heightened self-awareness, you recognize your irritation, understand its roots, and choose to respond calmly and constructively. This ability to pause, reflect, and then act appropriately can transform your personal and professional interactions.

Developing self-awareness begins with introspection. Setting aside regular time for reflection allows you to examine your thoughts, emotions, and behaviors. Journaling is a powerful tool for this purpose. By writing about your daily experiences and emotional reactions, you can identify patterns and triggers. For example, if you notice that certain situations consistently make you anxious, you can explore why this happens and how to address it. Reflective journaling not only provides insights into your emotional landscape but also helps track your progress over time.

Mindfulness meditation is another effective practice for cultivating self-awareness. It involves paying attention to the present moment without judgment. By focusing on your breath, physical sensations, or sounds around you, mindfulness helps quiet the mind and bring awareness to your internal state. Regular practice can increase your ability to observe your thoughts and emotions without becoming overwhelmed by them. Imagine sitting quietly for ten minutes each morning, simply noticing the flow of your thoughts. Over time, this practice can lead to a deeper understanding of your mental and emotional processes, enhancing your overall self-awareness.

Feedback from others is invaluable for gaining a more objective view of yourself. While self-reflection is crucial, it can be limited by personal biases. Seeking feedback from trusted friends, family members, or colleagues can provide different perspectives on your behavior and its impact. For instance, you might believe you handle stress well, but a colleague might point out that you become overly critical under pressure. This external input can highlight blind spots and areas for improvement. When seeking feedback, ask specific questions about your behavior and be open to constructive criticism. This openness not only fosters personal growth but also strengthens your relationships through increased trust and communication.

Another approach to developing self-awareness is through personality assessments. Tools like the Myers-Briggs Type Indicator (MBTI), the Big Five personality traits, or the Enneagram can offer insights into your personality, preferences, and behavioral tendencies. While these assessments are not definitive, they can provide a framework for understanding yourself better. For example, if an assessment reveals that you are highly introverted, you might be more aware of your need for solitude to recharge. Understanding your personality can help you make more informed decisions about your career, relationships, and lifestyle.

Emotional self-awareness, a subset of self-awareness, involves recognizing and understanding your own emotions. Emotions can be complex and multifaceted, often influencing our thoughts and actions in subtle ways. Developing emotional self-awareness requires paying attention to your feelings throughout the day. Start by labeling your emotions accurately. Instead of saying you feel "bad," try to pinpoint whether you feel angry, sad, frustrated, or anxious. This specificity can help you understand the underlying causes of your emotions and address them more effectively. For instance, if you identify that you are feeling anxious because of an upcoming presentation, you can take steps to prepare and manage your anxiety.

Understanding your values is a crucial aspect of self-awareness. Values are the principles and beliefs that guide your behavior and decision-making. They are deeply rooted in your upbringing, culture, and personal experiences. Reflecting on your values can help you understand why you prioritize certain aspects of your life and how they shape your actions. For example, if you value honesty, you might find it challenging to work in an environment where transparency is lacking. Identifying and aligning your actions with your values can lead to a more authentic and fulfilling life.

Self-awareness also involves recognizing your strengths and weaknesses. This understanding allows you to leverage your strengths and work on your weaknesses. Conduct a personal SWOT analysis (Strengths, Weaknesses, Opportunities, Threats) to gain a comprehensive view of your capabilities. For instance, if you identify that one of your strengths is effective communication, you can seek opportunities to use this skill more frequently, such as leading meetings or giving presentations. Conversely, if you recognize a weakness in time management, you can implement strategies to improve, such as setting specific goals and deadlines.

Setting aside time for regular self-reflection and assessment is essential for continuous growth. Consider scheduling a weekly review where you reflect on your experiences, achievements, and challenges. During this time, ask yourself questions like: What did I do well this week? What could I have done differently? What emotions did I experience, and why? This practice not only enhances self-awareness but also keeps you focused on your personal development goals.

Developing self-awareness is not a one-time effort but an ongoing process. Life's experiences, challenges, and changes continually shape your self-perception. Staying committed to self-awareness requires a willingness to adapt and grow. Embrace new experiences, seek feedback regularly, and remain open to learning about yourself. This dynamic approach to self-awareness ensures that you remain aligned with your evolving values, goals, and aspirations.

Self-awareness also plays a critical role in leadership. Leaders who are self-aware are better equipped to understand their impact on others, make informed decisions, and create a positive organizational culture. Imagine a leader who understands their tendency to become impatient under stress. By being aware of this, they can implement strategies to manage their impatience, such as taking breaks or delegating tasks. This self-regulation not only improves their effectiveness but also sets a positive example for their team.

In personal relationships, self-awareness fosters deeper connections and more effective communication. Being aware of your own emotions and triggers allows you to navigate conflicts more constructively. For instance, if you recognize that you feel defensive during arguments, you can take a step back and approach the situation with a more open and understanding mindset. This self-awareness can prevent misunderstandings and promote healthier, more empathetic interactions.

Developing self-awareness can also enhance your overall well-being. By understanding your emotional needs and triggers, you can implement strategies to manage stress, prevent burnout, and maintain a balanced lifestyle. For example, if you notice that you feel overwhelmed after long periods of social interaction, you can schedule regular alone time to recharge. This proactive approach to self-care ensures that you maintain your mental and emotional health.

Cultivating self-awareness involves a combination of introspection, mindfulness, feedback, and continuous learning. It requires a commitment to understanding and accepting yourself fully, with all your strengths and weaknesses. By developing self-awareness, you can enhance your emotional intelligence, improve your relationships, and achieve greater personal and professional fulfillment. This journey of self-discovery is a lifelong process, offering the potential for profound growth and transformation. As you deepen your self-awareness, you also become more attuned to how your internal state affects your external behavior. For example, recognizing how stress impacts your decision-making can help you develop healthier coping mechanisms. You might discover that taking short walks or practicing breathing exercises can significantly reduce your stress levels, leading to better choices and actions.

Managing Emotions Effectively

Managing emotions effectively is a crucial skill that influences every aspect of life, from personal well-being to professional success. Emotions, when properly managed, can enhance decision-making, improve relationships, and foster resilience. However, unmanaged emotions can lead to impulsive actions, strained interactions, and heightened stress. Developing emotional management skills involves understanding your emotions, recognizing their triggers, and employing strategies to navigate them constructively.

Imagine a scenario where you're preparing for an important presentation at work. As the date approaches, you start feeling anxious and overwhelmed. Without effective emotional management, this anxiety could escalate, potentially affecting your performance. However, by recognizing the onset of anxiety and employing techniques to manage it, such as deep breathing or visualization, you can maintain your composure and deliver a confident presentation.

Understanding your emotions is the first step in managing them. Emotions are complex and often arise from a combination of thoughts, experiences, and physiological responses. To effectively manage your emotions, start by identifying what you are feeling in the moment. Instead of labeling a general sense of discomfort as "bad," try to pinpoint whether you are feeling frustrated, nervous, or disappointed. This specificity allows you to address the root cause of your emotions more effectively.

One practical method for understanding your emotions is to keep an emotion journal. Document your feelings throughout the day, noting the situations that triggered them and your reactions. Over time, this practice can reveal patterns and help you anticipate emotional responses. For example, you might notice that you feel particularly stressed during team meetings. Recognizing this pattern allows you to prepare and implement strategies to manage your stress, such as practicing relaxation techniques beforehand.

Recognizing emotional triggers is key to managing your responses. Triggers can be external, such as specific situations or interactions, or internal, such as thoughts or memories. By identifying your triggers, you can develop strategies to mitigate their impact. Suppose you realize that criticism from colleagues triggers feelings of inadequacy. Understanding this can help you approach feedback with a more balanced perspective, focusing on constructive aspects rather than personal shortcomings.

Mindfulness is a powerful tool for managing emotions. It involves paying attention to the present moment without judgment, which can help you observe your emotions as they arise without becoming overwhelmed by them. Regular mindfulness practice can enhance your ability to respond to emotions thoughtfully rather than react impulsively. For instance, if you find yourself getting angry during a heated discussion, mindfulness can help you pause, take a deep breath, and respond calmly rather than lashing out.

Breathing exercises are another effective technique for managing emotions. Deep, slow breathing activates the parasympathetic nervous system, which promotes relaxation and reduces stress. When you feel emotionally charged, take a few moments to focus on your breath. Inhale deeply through your nose, hold for a few seconds, and exhale slowly through your mouth. This simple practice can help you regain control and approach the situation with a clearer mind.

Cognitive reframing is a strategy that involves changing the way you interpret situations to alter your emotional response. It requires identifying negative thought patterns and replacing them with more positive or balanced perspectives. For example, if you find yourself thinking, "I'll never be able to handle this project," reframe it to, "This project is challenging, but I have the skills and resources to manage it." This shift in perspective can reduce feelings of anxiety and increase your confidence.

Incorporating physical activity into your routine can also enhance emotional management. Exercise releases endorphins, which are natural mood lifters, and helps reduce stress hormones like cortisol. Regular physical activity can improve your overall emotional health, making it easier to manage emotions during challenging times. Whether it's a daily walk, a yoga session, or a more intense workout, find an activity that you enjoy and make it a part of your routine.

Social support is another critical element in managing emotions. Sharing your feelings with trusted friends, family members, or a therapist can provide valuable insights and emotional relief. Sometimes, simply talking about your emotions can help you process and understand them better. For example, discussing your feelings of frustration with a colleague might reveal underlying issues that you can address together, improving both your emotional state and your working relationship.

Setting healthy boundaries is essential for managing emotions effectively. Boundaries help protect your emotional well-being by ensuring that your needs and limits are respected. Learn to say no when necessary and prioritize activities that align with your values and goals. For instance, if you find that attending too many social events leaves you feeling drained, set a limit on how many you attend each month. This practice can help you maintain a healthy emotional balance.

Developing emotional resilience is an ongoing process that involves learning from experiences and adapting to challenges. Reflect on past situations where you managed your emotions effectively and those where you struggled. Identify the strategies that worked and consider how you can apply them in future scenarios. For example, if you handled a difficult conversation well by staying calm and focused, remember this approach for similar situations.

Emotional management also involves self-compassion, which means treating yourself with kindness and understanding during difficult times. Acknowledge your emotions without judgment and offer yourself the same support and encouragement you would give to a friend. For instance, if you feel disappointed after a setback, remind yourself that it's okay to feel this way and that setbacks are a natural part of growth.

In the workplace, managing emotions effectively can enhance your professional relationships and performance. Practice active listening during interactions with colleagues, which involves fully focusing on the speaker, understanding their message, and responding thoughtfully. This approach can prevent misunderstandings and reduce conflict. Additionally, manage workplace stress by taking regular breaks, setting realistic goals, and maintaining a healthy work-life balance.

In personal relationships, effective emotional management can deepen connections and improve communication. Be open and honest about your feelings, and encourage your loved ones to do the same. This transparency fosters trust and understanding. For example, if you feel hurt by a friend's comment, express your feelings calmly and constructively rather than letting resentment build up.

Managing emotions is not about suppressing or ignoring them but about understanding and navigating them in a healthy way. Embrace your emotions as a natural part of the human experience, and use them as a guide to make informed decisions and build stronger connections. By developing emotional management skills, you can enhance your overall well-being and lead a more fulfilling life.

In summary, managing emotions effectively involves a combination of self-awareness, mindfulness, cognitive reframing, physical activity, social support, and self-compassion. By understanding your emotions and their triggers, and employing strategies to navigate them constructively, you can improve your personal and professional life. This ongoing process of emotional management not only enhances your emotional intelligence but also empowers you to face challenges with resilience and confidence. Embrace this journey as an opportunity for growth and self-discovery, knowing that each step brings you closer to mastering your emotions and achieving your full potential. Effective emotional management is a lifelong endeavor that requires continuous learning and adaptation. Each experience you encounter, whether positive or negative, offers valuable lessons that can enhance your emotional intelligence and resilience. Embrace every opportunity to refine your skills and deepen your understanding of your emotional landscape.

Empathy and Understanding Your Partner

Empathy and understanding your partner are foundational to building and maintaining a healthy, fulfilling relationship. These qualities foster deep emotional connections, enhance communication, and create a supportive environment where both partners feel valued and respected. Developing empathy involves more than just recognizing your partner's feelings; it requires actively listening, validating their experiences, and responding with compassion.

Consider a scenario where your partner comes home visibly upset after a challenging day at work. Instead of offering immediate solutions or dismissing their feelings, you take a moment to listen attentively, acknowledging their emotions without judgment. This act of empathy not only provides emotional support but also strengthens the bond between you.

Active listening is a critical component of empathy. It involves fully engaging with your partner when they speak, giving them your undivided attention, and avoiding interruptions. This means putting away distractions, such as phones or laptops, and focusing entirely on your partner. When they see that you are genuinely interested in what they have to say, it fosters trust and openness in the relationship. Reflecting back what you've heard, through phrases like "It sounds like you're feeling..." or "I understand that you are...", can also validate their emotions and show that you are truly listening.

Understanding your partner requires a willingness to see the world from their perspective. This means considering their background, experiences, and individual temperament. Everyone has a unique way of interpreting situations based on their past experiences and personality traits. By acknowledging these differences, you can better appreciate why your partner feels or reacts the way they do. For example, if your partner tends to withdraw during conflicts, it might stem from a past where open confrontation led to negative outcomes. Recognizing this can help you approach conflicts with more sensitivity and patience.

Developing empathy also involves being aware of your own emotional responses and biases. Self-awareness allows you to manage your reactions and remain present for your partner. If you find yourself becoming defensive or dismissive during a conversation, take a moment to pause and reflect on why you are feeling that way. This self-regulation not only improves your ability to empathize but also sets a positive example for your partner.

Communication is another vital aspect of understanding your partner. Open and honest communication creates a safe space for both partners to express their thoughts and feelings. Regular check-ins, where you discuss your emotional states and any concerns, can prevent misunderstandings and foster a deeper connection. These conversations should be approached with a mindset of curiosity and non-judgment, allowing both partners to share openly without fear of criticism.

Consider using "I" statements during discussions to express your feelings without placing blame. For example, instead of saying, "You never listen to me," you might say, "I feel unheard when you look at your phone while I'm talking." This approach reduces defensiveness and opens the door to more constructive dialogue. By focusing on your own experiences, you can communicate your needs more effectively and encourage your partner to do the same.

Empathy extends beyond verbal communication. Nonverbal cues, such as body language and facial expressions, play a significant role in how we connect with others. Pay attention to your partner's nonverbal signals and respond appropriately. A comforting touch or a reassuring smile can convey empathy and support in powerful ways. Similarly, being mindful of your own nonverbal signals can help you communicate more effectively. Maintain eye contact, nod to show understanding, and use open body language to demonstrate your attentiveness.

Shared activities and experiences can also enhance understanding and empathy in a relationship. Engaging in activities that your partner enjoys, or trying new things together, can provide insights into their interests and values. These shared moments create opportunities for bonding and deepening your connection. Whether it's cooking a meal together, taking a walk, or exploring a new hobby, spending quality time with your partner strengthens your emotional ties and fosters mutual understanding.

Another important aspect of empathy is recognizing and respecting your partner's boundaries. Everyone has their limits, and honoring these boundaries is crucial for maintaining a healthy relationship. Encourage your partner to express their needs and preferences, and be willing to accommodate them. For instance, if your partner needs some alone time to recharge after a busy day, respect their request and give them the space they need. This respect for boundaries not only demonstrates empathy but also builds trust and respect in the relationship.

Conflict is inevitable in any relationship, but how you handle it can significantly impact your connection with your partner. Approach conflicts with a mindset of empathy and understanding, rather than defensiveness or blame. Try to understand your partner's perspective and acknowledge their feelings, even if you don't agree with them. This validation can de-escalate tensions and pave the way for more productive discussions. For example, if your partner is upset because they feel neglected, acknowledging their feelings and discussing ways to spend more quality time together can help resolve the issue more effectively than dismissing their concerns.

Empathy also involves being supportive during your partner's difficult times. Life is filled with challenges, and having a supportive partner can make a significant difference. Offer your support by listening, providing encouragement, and helping them find solutions. Whether it's a work-related stress, a personal loss, or a health issue, being there for your partner in times of need strengthens your bond and demonstrates your commitment to their well-being. For instance, if your partner is going through a tough period at work, offering to take on some household responsibilities or simply being a listening ear can show your empathy and support.

In addition to providing support, it's important to celebrate your partner's successes and achievements. Sharing in their joy and accomplishments fosters a positive and supportive relationship. Whether it's a promotion at work, completing a personal goal, or overcoming a challenge, acknowledging and celebrating these moments together strengthens your connection and reinforces your mutual appreciation.

Empathy and understanding are not static skills; they require ongoing effort and practice. Regularly reflect on how you can improve your empathetic responses and deepen your understanding of your partner. Seek feedback from your partner and be open to making adjustments. Relationships are dynamic, and continually striving to enhance your empathy and understanding will contribute to a more fulfilling and resilient partnership.

In summary, empathy and understanding are essential components of a healthy and thriving relationship. By practicing active listening, recognizing and respecting your partner's perspective, and communicating openly, you can foster a deeper emotional connection. Nonverbal communication, shared activities, and respecting boundaries further enhance your empathy and understanding. Handling conflicts with empathy and providing support during difficult times strengthens your bond and demonstrates your commitment to each other. Celebrating successes and continually striving to improve your empathetic responses contribute to a fulfilling and resilient partnership. Embrace these practices as part of your ongoing journey to build a strong, empathetic, and understanding relationship with your partner. Empathy and understanding are not just about the grand gestures or the significant conversations. They are woven into the fabric of daily interactions, small acts of kindness, and the way you respond to each other's needs on a routine basis. Taking the time to genuinely ask about your partner's day and listen to their response, offering a hug when they seem down, or even just making their favorite cup of coffee in the morning can all be powerful expressions of empathy and understanding.

Emotional Regulation Strategies

Emotional regulation is an essential skill for maintaining personal well-being and fostering healthy relationships. It involves managing and responding to your emotions in a way that is both constructive and appropriate. Emotional regulation doesn't mean suppressing or ignoring emotions; rather, it involves recognizing, understanding, and effectively managing your feelings. For beginners, developing emotional regulation strategies can significantly improve your ability to navigate life's challenges and maintain emotional balance.

One foundational strategy for emotional regulation is mindfulness. Mindfulness involves paying attention to the present moment without judgment. By practicing mindfulness, you can become more aware of your emotions as they arise, which allows you to respond to them thoughtfully rather than react impulsively. Simple mindfulness exercises, such as deep breathing, meditation, or body scans, can help you stay grounded and centered. For instance, if you find yourself feeling anxious or overwhelmed, taking a few minutes to focus on your breath can help calm your mind and reduce stress.

Another effective strategy is cognitive reappraisal, which involves changing the way you think about a situation to alter its emotional impact. This can be particularly helpful in reducing negative emotions and increasing positive ones. For example, if you receive constructive criticism at work, instead of viewing it as a personal failure, you can reframe it as an opportunity for growth and improvement. This shift in perspective can help you manage feelings of defensiveness or frustration and approach the feedback with a more open and positive attitude.

Developing a regular practice of self-reflection can also enhance your emotional regulation skills. Taking time to reflect on your emotions and the situations that trigger them can provide valuable insights into your emotional patterns and responses. Journaling is a practical tool for self-reflection. By writing about your experiences and feelings, you can identify recurring themes and develop a better understanding of your emotional landscape. This awareness can empower you to anticipate and manage your emotions more effectively in the future.

Physical activity is another powerful tool for regulating emotions. Exercise has been shown to reduce symptoms of anxiety and depression, improve mood, and increase overall emotional well-being. Engaging in regular physical activity, whether it's running, yoga, or dancing, can help release built-up tension and provide a healthy outlet for stress. Additionally, exercise stimulates the production of endorphins, which are natural mood elevators. Incorporating physical activity into your daily routine can create a positive impact on your emotional regulation.

Building a strong support network is crucial for emotional regulation. Surrounding yourself with supportive friends and family members can provide a valuable source of comfort and perspective during challenging times. When you share your feelings with trusted individuals, it can help you process your emotions and gain new insights. Social support not only helps buffer the effects of stress but also fosters a sense of belonging and connection. Don't hesitate to reach out to your support network when you need emotional support or guidance.

Practicing self-compassion is another essential strategy for emotional regulation. Self-compassion involves treating yourself with the same kindness and understanding that you would offer to a friend. When you experience difficult emotions or setbacks, it's important to avoid self-criticism and instead practice self-care and self-acceptance. For example, if you make a mistake, rather than berating yourself, acknowledge that everyone makes mistakes and use the experience as an opportunity for learning and growth. Cultivating self-compassion can help you manage negative emotions more effectively and maintain a balanced emotional state.

Time management and setting realistic goals can also play a significant role in emotional regulation. Feeling overwhelmed by a long to-do list or unrealistic expectations can lead to stress and frustration. By prioritizing tasks, breaking them into manageable steps, and setting achievable goals, you can reduce feelings of overwhelm and increase your sense of control. Effective time management helps create a more balanced and less stressful environment, which in turn supports better emotional regulation.

Developing healthy coping mechanisms is essential for managing difficult emotions. Unhealthy coping strategies, such as substance use or avoidance, can exacerbate emotional distress and lead to long-term negative consequences. Instead, focus on healthy coping mechanisms, such as engaging in hobbies, spending time in nature, or practicing relaxation techniques. For example, if you feel stressed, taking a walk in the park or spending time on a creative project can provide a healthy distraction and help you process your emotions.

Sleep hygiene is another important aspect of emotional regulation. Poor sleep can negatively impact your mood, cognitive function, and overall emotional well-being. Establishing a regular sleep routine, creating a restful sleep environment, and avoiding stimulants before bedtime can improve the quality of your sleep. Prioritizing good sleep hygiene helps ensure that you are well-rested and better equipped to manage your emotions effectively.

Learning to identify and label your emotions accurately is a key component of emotional regulation. Often, emotions can feel overwhelming or confusing, making it difficult to understand and manage them. By developing a rich emotional vocabulary and practicing emotional granularity, you can differentiate between subtle variations in your feelings. For example, instead of simply feeling "bad," you might identify that you feel "disappointed," "frustrated," or "anxious." This precise labeling helps you understand the root causes of your emotions and choose appropriate strategies for managing them.

In addition to these individual strategies, seeking professional help can be beneficial for those who struggle with emotional regulation. Therapists and counselors can provide valuable tools and techniques for managing emotions, as well as offer a supportive space to explore underlying issues. Cognitive-behavioral therapy (CBT), dialectical behavior therapy (DBT), and other therapeutic approaches are specifically designed to enhance emotional regulation skills. If you find that your emotions are consistently interfering with your daily life, professional guidance can be an important step toward better emotional health.

Developing emotional regulation skills is an ongoing process that requires practice and patience. It's important to remember that everyone experiences setbacks and challenges along the way. By consistently applying these strategies and being gentle with yourself, you can build resilience and improve your ability to manage your emotions. Over time, these skills will become more natural, helping you navigate life's ups and downs with greater ease and confidence.

Emotional regulation is a vital aspect of personal growth and well-being. By incorporating mindfulness, cognitive reappraisal, self-reflection, physical activity, social support, self-compassion, time management, healthy coping mechanisms, sleep hygiene, and professional help, you can develop effective strategies for managing your emotions. These skills not only enhance your emotional health but also contribute to more fulfilling and harmonious relationships. Embrace the journey of emotional regulation, and you will find greater balance, resilience, and overall well-being in your life. Emotional regulation is not just about managing negative emotions; it's also about fostering positive ones. Cultivating positive emotions can enhance your resilience and overall emotional health. One effective way to do this is through gratitude practice. Regularly reflecting on the things you are grateful for can shift your focus from what's lacking or problematic to what's abundant and positive in your life. Keeping a gratitude journal, where you write down a few things you are grateful for each day, can help reinforce this habit. This practice can lead to increased feelings of happiness and contentment, which in turn, make it easier to regulate your emotions during challenging times.

Conflict Resolution

Conflict is an inevitable part of human interaction. Whether in personal relationships, workplace settings, or social environments, disagreements and disputes arise when differing needs, values, and perspectives clash. Effective conflict resolution strategies are essential for managing these situations constructively, fostering understanding, and maintaining healthy relationships. The ability to resolve conflicts not only minimizes stress but also promotes a more harmonious and productive environment.

Understanding the nature of conflict is the first step towards resolving it. Conflict often stems from a variety of sources, including miscommunication, unmet needs, differing values, or competition for resources. Recognizing the underlying causes can provide valuable insights into how to address and resolve the issue. For instance, a workplace conflict might arise from unclear job roles or expectations, leading to frustration and misunderstandings. By identifying the root cause, you can tailor your resolution approach to address the specific issues at hand.

Active listening is a crucial skill in conflict resolution. It involves fully concentrating on the speaker, understanding their message, and responding thoughtfully. When both parties feel heard and understood, it creates a foundation for mutual respect and cooperation. To practice active listening, maintain eye contact, nod in acknowledgment, and avoid interrupting. Paraphrasing what the other person has said can also demonstrate that you are engaged and understand their perspective. For example, you might say, "So what I hear you saying is that you feel overwhelmed by the current workload and need more support."

Empathy plays a significant role in resolving conflicts. Empathy involves putting yourself in the other person's shoes and understanding their feelings and viewpoints. It helps to reduce defensiveness and promotes a more collaborative approach to finding a solution. For instance, if a friend is upset because they feel neglected, acknowledging their feelings by saying, "I can see why you feel hurt; I haven't been as available lately," can help de-escalate the situation and open the door to constructive dialogue.

Effective communication is essential for resolving conflicts. Clear, direct, and respectful communication can prevent misunderstandings and ensure that both parties' needs and concerns are addressed. Using "I" statements instead of "you" statements can help avoid blame and reduce defensiveness. For example, saying "I feel frustrated when the deadlines are not met" is more constructive than "You never meet the deadlines." This approach focuses on expressing your own feelings and needs rather than criticizing the other person.

Finding common ground is another effective strategy for conflict resolution. Identifying shared goals or interests can create a sense of teamwork and cooperation. For instance, in a workplace conflict over project responsibilities, both parties might agree that the primary goal is to ensure the project's success. By focusing on this common objective, they can work together to find a solution that satisfies both parties. This might involve redistributing tasks, improving communication, or seeking additional resources.

Compromise and negotiation are often necessary when resolving conflicts. This involves finding a middle ground where both parties can make concessions to reach a mutually acceptable solution. Effective negotiation requires flexibility and a willingness to consider the other person's needs and perspectives. For example, if two colleagues are in conflict over office space, they might negotiate a rotating schedule or agree to share the space in a way that accommodates both of their needs.

Setting clear boundaries can help prevent conflicts from escalating. Boundaries define acceptable behavior and ensure that both parties' needs and limits are respected. For instance, in a personal relationship, setting boundaries about personal time and space can prevent feelings of suffocation or neglect. Clearly communicating these boundaries and consistently enforcing them can create a healthier and more respectful interaction.

Problem-solving skills are essential for resolving conflicts constructively. This involves identifying the problem, generating possible solutions, evaluating the options, and implementing the chosen solution. A structured problem-solving approach can help both parties stay focused on finding a resolution rather than getting bogged down in emotional reactions. For example, if roommates are in conflict over household chores, they could brainstorm a list of potential solutions, such as creating a chore schedule or hiring a cleaning service, and then decide together on the best option.

Sometimes, conflicts cannot be resolved without the help of a neutral third party. Mediation involves bringing in an impartial mediator who can facilitate the discussion and help both parties reach a resolution. Mediators are trained to manage conflicts and can provide valuable guidance and support. This approach is especially useful in more complex or emotionally charged conflicts where direct communication has proven ineffective. For instance, in family disputes or legal conflicts, a mediator can help navigate the discussions and work towards a fair and balanced resolution.

It is also important to manage your own emotions during a conflict. Strong emotions such as anger, frustration, or hurt can cloud judgment and escalate the situation. Techniques such as deep breathing, taking a break, or practicing mindfulness can help you stay calm and composed. For instance, if you feel yourself getting angry during a conflict, stepping away for a few minutes to collect your thoughts can prevent an emotional outburst and allow you to approach the discussion more rationally.

Reflecting on past conflicts and their resolutions can provide valuable lessons for future interactions. Consider what strategies worked well and what could have been handled differently. This reflection can help you develop a more nuanced understanding of conflict dynamics and improve your conflict resolution skills over time. For example, if you realize that a previous conflict was resolved through effective communication and compromise, you might prioritize these strategies in future disputes.

In any conflict, it is crucial to maintain a focus on the relationship rather than just the issue at hand. Preserving the relationship and ensuring that both parties feel respected and valued can lead to more sustainable and positive outcomes. This might involve acknowledging the other person's contributions, expressing appreciation, and finding ways to strengthen the relationship even as you work through the conflict. For instance, after resolving a conflict with a colleague, you might suggest working on a new project together to rebuild trust and collaboration.

Ultimately, effective conflict resolution requires a combination of skills and strategies. By understanding the nature of conflict, practicing active listening and empathy, communicating effectively, finding common ground, compromising, setting boundaries, problem-solving, seeking mediation when necessary, managing emotions, reflecting on past experiences, and focusing on relationships, you can navigate conflicts more effectively and constructively. These skills not only help resolve individual disputes but also contribute to a more positive and harmonious environment in all areas of your life.

Conflict resolution is an ongoing process that requires patience, practice, and a commitment to continuous improvement. By applying these principles consistently, you can develop the ability to manage conflicts with greater ease and confidence, ultimately leading to stronger and more fulfilling relationships. One important aspect of conflict resolution is the ability to recognize when to disengage temporarily. There are times when continuing a discussion may only exacerbate tensions and lead to more entrenched positions. Knowing when to take a step back can be crucial for allowing emotions to cool and for both parties to reflect on the situation. For example, if a conversation is becoming increasingly heated, suggesting a break and agreeing to reconvene after a set period can help both parties regain composure and approach the problem with a clearer mind.